资金支持：北京中医药大学基本科研业务费项目（2023-JYB-HZZ-002）

Empirical Study on the Training Strategy of English Major Graduate Students in China

中国英语专业研究生培养策略实证研究

王 曦 著

中国海洋大学出版社
· 青岛 ·

图书在版编目(CIP)数据

中国英语专业研究生培养策略实证研究 / 王曦著 . 青岛：中国海洋大学出版社，2024. 7. -- ISBN 978-7-5670-3901-8

Ⅰ. H319. 3

中国国家版本馆 CIP 数据核字第 20242YS009 号

出版发行	中国海洋大学出版社		
社　　址	青岛市香港东路 23 号	邮政编码	266071
出 版 人	刘文菁		
网　　址	http://pub.ouc.edu.cn		
订购电话	0532－82032573（传真）		
责任编辑	邵成军	电　　话	0532－85902533
印　　制	青岛国彩印刷股份有限公司		
版　　次	2024 年 7 月第 1 版		
印　　次	2024 年 7 月第 1 次印刷		
成品尺寸	170 mm ×230 mm		
印　　张	10.75		
字　　数	196 千		
印　　数	1—1 000		
定　　价	79. 00 元		

总序（一）

中国海洋大学出版社将国内外国语言学及应用语言学博士研究生的优秀论文集中出版建立文库，对学界来说是件极好的事。目前已经出版了第一辑总计15本专著，在学界引起了很大的反响和广泛的关注。现在，第二辑论文专著正在筹划与编辑中。希望挑选出来的优秀博士学位论文能够丰富该文库的学术内容，促进该领域的学术争鸣。

作为一门学科，外国语言学及应用语言学涉及面极为广泛，几乎包罗万象。因此，要规划好第二辑论文主题，先要对该学科有个明确的范围界定，以期有的放矢地挑选相关的优秀论文。

外国语言学及应用语言学，顾名思义，是指与外国语言紧密相关的语言研究学说及用来解释语言问题的相关理论。这样界定似乎较为完整，但仔细分析发现，其中存在着概念界定模糊、内容划分不明等问题。

首先，学科名称"外国语言学及应用语言学"就值得商榷。外国语言学是个大概念，其他的语言学分支包含其中，如心理语言学、社会语言学、应用语言学，不应把语言学和其分支并列作为学科名称。因此，外国语言学及应用语言学似有概念混淆之嫌。其次，语言学有国内国外之分虽也说得过去，但叫常造成共性语言现象研究的归类困难。而且应用语言学因涉及领域过于广泛而很难界定其确切的研究范围。当然，现在外国语言学及应用语言学作为学科名称已约定俗成，人们心目中也已经有了一个大概的范畴，但鉴于中国海洋大学出版社要出版此学科的第二辑博士学位论文专著，理应对这一学科有一个理性的解读。

语言学的研究（无论国内国外），大致分为理论层面的研究和应用层面的研究。理论层面的研究主要集中于对语言的描述以及人类语言的普遍规律或语言与某一领域的结合，如语音研究有音位学，词汇研究有词汇学，句子研究有句法学，还有语法学；与某一领域结合起来的研究有心理语言学、社会语言学、神经语言学、计算语言学、系统功能语言学等。应用层面的研究又可以分为宏观、中观和微观三个研究视角。宏观研究视角主要与语言政策及语言教育政策的研究有关，如语言的地位规划、语言的本体规划、语言的习得规划以及教育上使用何种语言等问题。中观研究视角大多关注语言在社会生活中的使用，如语言的翻译、语言的社会交际、语言的态度、专门领域中的语言使用以及方言、民族语言和外国语言的和谐共存与发展。而微观研究视角与外语教育教学有关，包括语言课程、教学方法、教学大纲、课堂教学、信息技术与外语教学、教育技术与外语教学等。综上所述，外国语言学及应用语言学与语言的理论研究和应用研究息息相关，并涉及上述的方方面面。

可见，学科研究范围的解读界定了博士文库所包含的内容。第一辑的 15 本博士论文专著主要涵盖两个方面：语言本体研究与语言教学研究，符合学科的理论研究和应用研究。即将出版的第二辑博士学位论文专著，除了涵盖第一辑的研究内容外，其研究焦点应集中在以下几个方面：语言和认知的结合、语言的普遍规律、语言的变化与发展（理论层面）；语言政策与语言规划、课程开发与课堂教学、信息技术与语言教学、“互联网＋”语言教学解决方案（应用层面）等。

博士文库的建立主要是为了把相关领域的最新研究成果集中展示，供人参考、研究和借鉴。因此，必须体现文库的开放性、内容的完整性、论述的创新性以及研究的科学性。这样才能充分发挥博士文库应有的学术价值！

中国海洋大学出版社以先进的编辑理念和敏锐的学术意识策划并设计了外国语言学及应用语言学博士文库，为广大的优秀博士人才提供了展示自己学术研究成果的交流平台。相信博士文库的不断丰富和完善，必将极大地促进该领域的研究和发展。

陈坚林

上海外国语大学教授、博士生导师

《外语电化教学》主编

总序（二）

在我国外语研究中，语言学自20世纪80年代后期开始蓬勃发展，先是作为英语语言文学、日语语言文学、俄语语言文学等二级学科的一个研究方向，之后外国语言学及应用语言学被列为外国语言文学一级学科下面的二级学科。当前，在外语语言学方面具有较强实力的院校一般拥有数个二级学科或一级学科。语言学蓬勃发展的另一个表现是研究生培养规模的扩大。90年代初，语言学硕士研究生还不多，博士研究生更是凤毛麟角。当时招博士研究生的只有北大、北外、上外、广外等院校，招生人数也是屈指可数。后来，增设外语博士点的院校数量稳步增加，现在招收外语语言学博士研究生的院校已经超过40所，每年招生人数在200人左右，学制一般为3～4年，最长不超过8年。随着高校对外语教师水平和学历要求的不断提高，广大教师考博的热情高涨，20余人竞争1个名额已属常见。报考语言学方面的博士研究生一般需要对语言学有一定的兴趣和热情，硕士研究生阶段已打下较好的基础，其后能经常研读相关学刊，最好有1篇或数篇较高质量的论文在外语类核心期刊上发表。被录取后，通常要刻苦钻研，潜心修炼。其博士学位论文要经过开题、预答辩、盲审、答辩等严格环节，所以往往具有较高水平，甚至能达到国内外的领先水平。对个人来说，博士学位论文也代表了学术生涯的一个高峰，其后要超越并非易事。正是因为博士学位论文的质量较高，对其加工出版能有效促进学术发展，国内外出版界也时常为之。这些以博士论文为基础的专著经常能为出版社赢得美誉。

在过去10多年间，国内几家出版社，如河南大学出版社、上海交通大学出版社、科学出版社、陕西师范大学出版社、中国海洋大学（简称中国海大）出版社出版了一系列外语方面的博士学位论文，其中有很大一部分属于语言学，产生了良好的影响。其中，中国海大出版社自2008年开始重视外语语言学研究，建立了外国语言学及应用语言学博士文库，共计15本，并通过多种方式进行推广，产生了良好的社会效益。

近几年来，我因工作关系与中国海大出版社邵成军老师交往较多。2015 年下半年，邵老师打电话与我商量，想对外语语言学博士学位论文进行新的策划，后商定为“外国语言学及应用语言学博士文库（第二辑）”，以国内高质量的相关博士论文为对象，为专业性开放式学术系列，旨在为广大外语教师和研究生呈上丰盛的学术大餐。这套文库具有以下特点：① 加强策划——限定选题范围，请知名学者作序，统一开本、封面，加强后期宣传等；② 严把质量——对申请出版的博士论文呈送两位相关领域的专家进行指导，以进一步提高其学术水平；③ 精心编辑——由专业编辑对书稿进行高质量的编辑，确保其文字无差错，体例与规范等符合国家的出版要求；④ 立体推广——文库的专著出版后会通过书目推送、网络营销、会议赠送、撰写书评等多种方式向广大读者推介。

对广大外语教师和研究生来说，仔细阅读这套文库，将会在以下方面获益匪浅。

第一，能快速了解某一专题的国内外研究现状。博士学位论文要求有创新，前提是对国内外相关研究了如指掌。因此，通过答辩的博士学位论文的文献综述部分通常会对国内外相关论著进行梳理，并有的放矢地进行批判性评论。阅读这一部分可以使读者快速掌握某一专题的最新情况，为自己今后开展相关研究打下初步基础。

第二，了解所读专著的创新之处及创新思路。细读作者在对前人研究评论后所提出的研究内容、思路以及具体研究方法，可以窥见作者为什么选定某一专题的某个侧面，用什么理论框架及原因，研究方法有何创新等。了解这些内容并思考背后的原因能帮助读者提升在研究选题方面的功力，而好的选题对高质量研究而言是第一步。

第三，独立思考，发现其不足。阅读专著仅仅停留在吸收知识层面是不够的，还要对所读内容进行批判性思考。孔子也说过“学而不思则罔，思而不学则殆”，强调了思考的重要性。我们阅读专著时，只怀着学习的态度是不够的，还要有质疑和批判精神。可以思考以下问题：选题是否有意义？理论框架是否能为研究内容服务？受试是否有代表性？数据收集方法是否可靠？统计分析方法是否恰当？是否对结果进行了深入讨论？能否较好地解释所得出的结论？只有通过思考，发现所读专著存在的不足，我们才能在今后研究中予以克服，加以超越，学术才能发展。就阅读方法而言，读者适当关注博士学位论文的最后一章往往有事半功倍之效，因为作者通常会在该部分指出其研究的不足，并对以后的研究进行展望。

第四,写书评与综述,并进行原创研究。读了一本专著及相关论文,有些收获,对某个专题产生了兴趣,这是非常难得的。此时宜趁热打铁,有所行动。比较容易入手的是对所读专著撰写书评,写好后既可以向期刊投稿,也可以在网络上发布。此后,应进一步阅读相关文献,特别是最新论文,针对该专题撰写综述性论文。综述性论文要写好并不容易,首先选题要有意义,其次要具备全面性、逻辑性、批判性,若能适当采用一些新方法,如元分析、CiteSpace 软件,往往显得不落俗套。前两步只是做学问的"练手"步骤,更重要的是做原创研究,这最能体现一个学者的水平和贡献。原创研究一般具备以下特点:选题新、方法新、结论新,但如何实现要靠自己的琢磨与钻研,"纸上得来终觉浅,绝知此事要躬行"。

在中国海大出版社推出"外国语言学及应用语言学博士文库(第二辑)"之际,我应约作序,很是惶恐,同时也为这份信任所感动,遂不揣浅陋,与大家分享一点治学的体会。

蔡金亭
上海财经大学教授、博士生导师
《第二语言学习研究》主编

· Table of Contents ·

Chapter 1
Introduction

1.1 Rationale of the Study

In the context of China's English major programs, the graduate degree research paper and viva (oral examination) are important parts of their degree assessment. This assessment method is commonly used to evaluate the students' knowledge, research skills, and ability to articulate their ideas in English. During the assessment, students are typically questioned by a panel of professors or experts in the field, who assess their understanding of the subject matter, the quality of their research, and their overall academic ability.

The graduate degree assessment plays a crucial role in determining the students' final grades and their eligibility for obtaining their degree. It is important for students to demonstrate their expertise and academic capabilities in the field of English during the assessment.

However, there are several problems that can be identified in China's English major graduate degree assessment. There is a lack of standardized guidelines and criteria for evaluating English major graduate degree viva in China. This leads to inconsistency in the evaluation process and outcomes, as different universities and examiners may have different expectations and standards. The viva often focuses heavily on the candidate's English language proficiency rather than their research abilities and knowledge. This puts non-native English speakers at a disadvantage, as their language skills may be evaluated more critically than their research competence.

The viva often focuses solely on the candidate's thesis or dissertation, neglecting other important aspects of their academic and research abilities. This narrow focus limits the holistic evaluation of the candidate's overall capabilities and potential. The feedback provided to candidates after the assessment is vague and lacks specific guidance for improvement in many cases. This hinders the candidate's professional development as they may not receive adequate guidance to enhance their research skills. The assessment format of the viva can vary significantly across universities and even among different departments within the same institution. This lack of consistency makes it difficult to ensure fairness and transparency in the evaluation process. This research is conducted to cite references to substantiate facts to address the research problem.

The research intends to provide recommendations based on the findings and an innovative intervention plan will be designed for the enhancement of the graduate students' research output and performance.

1.2 Statement of the Problem

This study sought to assess the research performance of English major graduate students in selected Beijing universities, for an enhancement through an intervention plan.

Specifically, this study answered the following questions:

(1) What is the research performance of the graduate students in terms of: 1) research paper output; and 2) research defense based on viva standards?

(2) What are the significant factors affecting the research paper/output as perceived by the: 1) graduate students; and 2) panel members?

(3) What are the significant factors affecting the oral defense performance as perceived by the: 1) graduate students; and 2) panel members?

(4) Is there a significant relationship between the research performance of the students and the identified factors by themselves and the oral examiners?

(5) What innovative intervention plan may be designed for the enhancement of

the research output and defense performance?

1.3 Significance of the Study

This study has significant implications from three perspectives.

1.3.1 English Major Graduate Degree Students

This research study enhances the understanding of the assessment process, criteria, and supervision style for China's English major graduate degree students. This understanding not only benefits their learning and research, but also reduces their stress and improves their performance in the assessment.

1.3.2 English Major Graduate Degree Supervisors/Examiners

It provides an opportunity for China's graduate degree supervisors/examiners to learn from each other and reflect on their own assessment practices. By improving the policies and standards in graduate degree assessment, there will be fewer instances of academic misconduct and better study outcomes.

1.3.3 English Major Graduate Degree Programs

Based on the discussions of strategies to promote graduate degree student research performance among China's English major graduate degree programs, an innovation plan will be proposed. It is hoped that this plan will attract attention from the Chinese educational system and contribute to the development of a higher quality graduate research education mode in China, creating an excellent academic environment that is collaborative and competitive on a global scale.

1.4 Review of Related Literature

This part presents a literature review that is divided into three main parts. The first part of the literature review focuses on providing an explanation of key terms and theories related to graduate degree supervision and assessment. It aims to connect these assessments with important educational issues such as formative and summative assessment, learner attitudes and motivation, teacher-student relationships, the appropriate degree of autonomous learning, creatitivy and critical thinking. By exploring these connections, the review prompts us to reflect on the role that supervition and assessment play to promote graduate students' research performance.

The second part of the literature review focuses on the legal foundation of graduate degree assessment, including the process and policies in China. As the key content of the study, it introduces a framework for conducting the evaluation in a structured and systematic manner. It allows for the identification of areas for enhancement and the implementation of necessary changes to ensure the effectiveness and relevance of the evaluation process.

Lastly, it discusses the research conducted on the graduate degree assessment both within China and internationally. This section provides an overview of the various research studies conducted in this area, highlighting the diversity in processes, criteria, supervision, and people's differing perspectives on graduate degree assessment.

1.4.1 Theories

Based on the aforementioned research studies, several noteworthy theories can be identified in relation to the graduate degree viva. These theories encompass different assessment approaches, motivation, teacher-student relationships, learner autonomy, creativity, and critical thinking. These theories offer valuable insights and guidance for the implementation and supervision of graduate degree assessments in China's English major programs.

1.4.1.1 Assessment Approaches

According to Black and William (1998), assessment is an activity in which teachers assist students in their learning process and evaluate their progress. Furthermore, teachers can also use assessment to influence students. There are two main approaches to assessment: formative assessment, which emphasizes learning, and summative assessment, which focuses on grading. Boston (2002) pointed out that the tasks involved in these two approaches are quite distinct, and formative assessment has the potential to generate significant learning gains. McDowell (1996) argued that the most effective assessment methods encourage students to engage in deep learning with a genuine interest in the subject matter.

In traditional summative assessment, it is commonly believed that the majority of students fall within the normal range of performance, while only a few stand out.

As a result, there is a need to advocate for a new approach to assessment. Formative assessment, unlike traditional summative assessment, aims not to compare students within a group, but rather to foster motivation and learning.

Academics tend to view the graduate degree assessment as having a formative role, as they believe it offers examiners an opportunity to provide advice and guidance to candidates (Jackson & Tinkler, 2001). On the other hand, candidates themselves do not prioritize this formative element when it comes to the graduate degree assessment. In contrast, candidates are inclined to view the viva as a form of summative assessment, evaluating their academic knowledge in their field of study and the credibility of their thesis. Jackson and Tinkler (2001) attributed this difference in perception to the candidates' personal experiences during their viva. They argued that a negative viva experience can lead to anxiety, which can ultimately undermine performance.

The contrasting perspectives between students and academics regarding the assessment in British studies provide valuable insights for the Chinese context. Therefore, this study is of great significance as it seeks to investigate the role of assessments in China's English major graduate degree programs, with the intention of implementing improvements.

1.4.1.2 Motivation and Attitudes

The significance of motivation in students' learning has been emphasized a lot (Dörnyei, 2007). Brown (2007) has provided various perspectives on motivation, including the behavioral definition that emphasizes rewards as reinforcement for specific behaviors, the cognitive definition that highlights innate drive and self-reward, and the constructivist definition that considers the social context and personal choices. Dai and Sternberg (2004) made a distinction between intrinsic and extrinsic motivation. Brown (2007) defined intrinsic motivation as the internal enjoyment and satisfaction derived from engaging in learning activities, while extrinsic motivation refers to external regulation influenced by the social context.

Numerous studies on motivation have shown a strong preference for intrinsic drives. Drawing from previous research on hierarchy of needs, Murray, Gao, and Lamb (2011) argued that intrinsic motivation is superior to extrinsic motivation. Similarly, Dörnyei and Ushioda (2009) asserted that autonomy and self-rewards are more effective than rewards and punishments.

However, according to research conducted in Britain, the current graduate degree assessment places a significant amount of pressure on students. Both successful and unsuccessful candidates have expressed negative opinions about the process. In fact, some successful candidates have even described the viva experience as "destructive" and compared it to a "court martial" (Wallace, 2003). This undermines graduate students' research performance.

Chen (2014) discovered China's English major graduate students generally exhibit strong learning motivation, with extrinsic motivation surpassing intrinsic motivation. Their primary motivation for choosing to pursue a graduate degree in English comes from external incentives, such as securing a good job after graduation. Among these motivations, academic interest is the lowest.

It is evident that promoting intrinsic motivation is crucial in the context of graduate degree education in China. The emotional well-being of students should be given more attention, and their holistic interests should be emphasized. The present study, which investigates the pressure and emotional needs of English major graduate students in assessment, holds significance in fostering their intrinsic motivation towards research.

1.4.1.3 Teacher-student Relationship

Many studies have examined the significance of the teacher-student relationship. It has been found that a positive teacher-student relationship can enhance students' engagement in school, overall well-being, and academic achievements. Conversely, a negative relationship can impede students' learning progress (Spilt et al., 2011). They also highlighted the benefits both teachers and students can derive from a healthy teacher-student relationship.

Craney-Gallagher and Mayer (2006) have identified recognition, familiarity, respect, and commitment as key elements of a good teacher-student relationship. Riddle (2003) has also emphasized the importance of effective communication and discipline in fostering a positive teacher-student relationship. Several scholars have conducted research on the teacher-student relationship in Chinese universities.

Huang and Yao (2006) examined the historical development of the teacher-student relationship in Chinese universities, advocating for close democratic relationships within a free academic atmosphere. Zhang (2012) conducted an analysis on the disharmony between teachers and students, attributing it to various factors including the behavior of both teachers and students, as well as their interactions. Additionally, Huang and Yao (2006) emphasized the impact of the social and academic environment on shaping teacher-student relationships.

Hence, in order to establish a positive teacher-student relationship that mutually benefits both parties, it requires collective efforts from all perspectives. However, in the context of China's graduate degree assessment, the impact of the teacher-student relationship on students' academic achievement remains largely unexplored.

Research has found that research self-efficacy and professional commitment play partial mediating roles between teacher-student relationship and adaptation to graduate degree study. Research self-efficacy and professional commitment also have a chain mediating effect on the relationship between teacher-student relationship and adaptation to graduate degree study. This means that teacher-student relationship not only directly influences the learning adaptation of graduate degree students but also indirectly affects it through research self-efficacy and professional commitment (Xin et al., 2023).

Only a few studies on viva supervision partially reflect the teacher-student relationship. For instance, Gu and Chen (2011) examined the varying supervision styles and evaluation criteria in China's current graduate degree viva, highlighting the contrasting teacher-student relationships that exist among different viva supervisors and candidates. This indicates that some relationships may be characterized by closeness, while others may be more distant.

Gu and Chen (2011) also discussed instances of academic misconduct in China's graduate degree viva, which can arise due to the practice of inviting external examiners by the supervisors. As can be seen, the teacher-student relationship in China's graduate degree viva is shaped by academic pressures and societal expectations, as the success of students is closely tied to the success of their supervisors.

The present study focuses on investigating the teacher-student relationship in China's graduate degree education specifically within the English major. This research aims to provide additional evidence and support for the improvement of graduate degree education, ultimately contributing to its overall success.

1.4.1.4 Learner Autonomy

The concept of learner autonomy holds significant importance in the field of teaching and learning. As stated by Holec, (1981), learner autonomy refers to the capability of learners to assume responsibility for their own learning. This definition highlights the fundamental belief that learner autonomy is reliant on the learners themselves, rather than external learning circumstances (Dickinson, 1987).

Nevertheless, Little (2007) raised concerns about Holec's limited exploration of the psychological aspects of learner autonomy and argued that learners' ability to manage their learning is not inherently innate, but rather requires some form of guidance. Little (2000) emphasized that autonomy in language learning is contingent upon the development of learners' capacities to detach, critically reflect, make decisions, monitor progress, and evaluate their own learning processes.

Achieving consensus on the appropriate level of autonomy in the context of learner autonomy remains a challenge for subsequent studies exploring its potential meanings, as observed by Benson (2007). Nevertheless, numerous studies conducted in China have also highlighted the practical applications of learner autonomy, with several recommended teaching strategies proving to be insightful and invaluable.

As an illustration, Chen and Liu (2008) concentrated on college English teaching and proposed that teachers encourage students to develop their own study plans. They also emphasized the advantages of self-monitoring and evaluation. These strategies for fostering learner autonomy, which greatly contribute to students' learning, have the potential to significantly benefit China's graduate degree education if implemented appropriately.

There are some researches on students' research performance and learner autonomy in China's English major graduate degree programs. Liang, Yi, and Xia (2024) found that the graduate stage emphasizes the importance of graduate students' autonomous learning, requiring learners to maintain a positive learning attitude and self-discipline in order to achieve their desired learning goals.

However, the willingness and self-discipline of graduate students can be influenced by various factors. The communication skills of graduate students play a facilitating role in promoting autonomous learning, enhancing their level of effort, and ultimately improving academic achievement, especially within a learning team setting.

As mentioned earlier, the relationship between learner autonomy, supervision, and viva success is of great importance. Therefore, this study aims to investigate the current supervision practices, analyze their strengths and weaknesses, and determine an optimal level of learner autonomy. By doing so, it will provide valuable insights and recommendations for improving supervision methods to foster the development of students' learner autonomy. By doing so, the effectiveness of supervision in China's English major graduate degree programs can be enhanced. This will enable students to not only acquire academic knowledge but also cultivate their awareness and ability to seek knowledge independently. These outcomes hold great significance for their future studies and research endeavors.

1.4.1.5 Creativity and Critical Thinking

Creativity and critical thinking are important theories for graduate degree. Creativity and critical thinking ability can be traced back over 2,500 years to the ancient Greek period. The term "critical" originates from the Greek word "kriticos" and has the meaning of asking questions, understanding, and discernment. Dewey (1951), the founder of modern critical thinking, proposed that the intellectual goal of education is to shape people's habits of careful, clear, and thorough thinking.

Shi (2023) believed that the essence of graduates is to explore and create new knowledge through scientific research, and the exploration of new knowledge must rely on critical thinking logic. An important part of college and graduate-level education is developing critical analysis skills and methods that enable innovative research.

Yan (2018) also believed that academic innovation is the fundamental significance of scientific research and an important goal of talent cultivation in higher education. The widespread occurrence of phenomena such as "blindly following trends", "excessive reliance on reference materials", and "parroting others' opinions" in the translation of graduate dissertations highlights a severe lack of innovative ability. Only by guiding students to read mainstream literature extensively, acknowledging cultural differences between the East and the West, enhancing philosophical reasoning abilities, can students grasp the forefront of their disciplines, establish cultural confidence, strengthen critical thinking abilities, and ultimately enhance their academic innovation capabilities.

Zhou and Han (2022) found that the critical thinking skills of English major graduate students are at a moderate level. The main reasons for this are the lack of emphasis by schools, teachers' lack of problem awareness, and insufficient student engagement in learning. Strategies are proposed at the levels of schools, teachers, and students to enhance the critical thinking level of English major graduate students.

Du (2023) found that English major graduate students are able to effectively apply analytical and evaluative thinking skills but still need improvement in their reasoning abilities. The study suggests that this may be due to a lack of researcher identity recognition, a failure to develop independent thinking abilities, and a lack of motivation in learning. According to the research of Zhang (2013), it can be seen from the problems exposed by China's English major graduate students that insufficient academic innovation ability and literature review lacks speculative thinking are main problems in the development of their academic abilities.

Therefore, creativity and critical thinking ability need to be enhanced in the graduate degree cultivation. The evaluation and cultivation of creativity and critical thinking abilities in graduate thesis research and defense have profound implications for individual development, academic progress, and the advancement of knowledge. By emphasizing these skills, educational institutions can contribute to the production of well-rounded graduates who are equipped to tackle complex challenges and make significant contributions to their disciplines.

1.4.2 Previous Studies

Graduate degree assessment has been studied a lot in the world, including China. Previous studies can provide insights into the best practices followed in different countries and institutions. By examining these studies, graduate programs can identify effective approaches to conducting assessment and ensure that their own processes align with established standards.

Research on the assessment process can help identify areas where improvements can be made. It can shed light on the strengths and weaknesses of the existing system, allowing for modifications that enhance the fairness, rigor, and transparency of the examination. Studies on the assessment policies can also provide evidence-based insights that inform policy decisions related to graduate education. Policymakers can use this research to develop guidelines and regulations that ensure consistency and quality in the examination process. By understanding the assessment process in different contexts, graduate programs can improve their own practices and enhance the overall quality of graduate education. This can lead to better-prepared graduates who contribute meaningfully to their fields of study.

1.4.2.1 Previous International Studies

All around the world, there are lots of researches related to the assessment of graduate research theses (Prins et al., 2015). The published research relates to issues such as methods (Golding et al., 2014) and outcomes (Lovat et al., 2015). Although viva forms an important part of the graduate degree education, its necessity has often been questioned (Kiley et al., 2018).

Gould (2016) suggests that, as the graduate education develops into new forms and with pressures for some forms of standardization globally, alternative assessment processes might need to be implemented. In most of the UK literature related to thesis examination and research supervision, there is extensive discussion of opportunities for the candidate to practice for the viva situation. These learning opportunities are additional to regular seminars in the department, as well as presentations at national and international conferences (Sharmini, Spronken-Smith, Golding, & Harland, 2014). Smith (2014) also described an integrated part of the examination process normally restricted to the candidate and the examination panel, a process most germane to the tradition in England. Chen (2014) describes the process in one Canadian university which is a semi-public event wherein the candidate can invite a small number of colleagues, family and friends to attend as observers, with a total number of participants being 10-12 persons.

Taking into account the Australian Graduate Research Good Practice Principles, developed by the Australian Council of Graduate Research (ACGR, 2016), and referred to by most universities, in terms of the formal examination, the candidate might (or might not) be given some opportunity to discuss potential examiners some time prior to submission.

The Australian Qualifications Framework Council (2013, p.64) suggests that one of the many qualities graduates should have is: "Communication skills to explain and critique theoretical propositions, methodologies and conclusions, as well as communication skills to present cogently a complex investigation of originality or original research for external examination against international standards and to communicate results to peers and community."

While the national review of Higher Degree by Research (HDR) education in Australia, colloquially called the ACOLA Review (McGagh et al., 2016) found that: "Many stakeholders considered that the Australian research training system would benefit from greater emphasis being placed on the assessment of the candidate and the skills gained, rather than focus predominately on the assessment of the thesis" (p. xvi) no specific recommendation was made regarding the introduction of viva.

Scholars believed viva has both positive roles and negative roles. People realized that candidate misunderstanding and/or lack of knowledge of the purpose, processes and policies relating to the viva can contribute to the levels of anxiety often reported in the literature (Bassnett, 2014). Previous study also involved the coding framework that was extended to capture all reference to the viva and a new framework established to code the de-identified and transcribed interviews. From English language perspective, a sub-set of reports was analyzed, using a linguistic analysis approach "to better understand the evaluative language used in the reports" (Starfield et al., 2015, p. 130).

1.4.2.2 Previous Chinese Studies

In China, the graduate degree viva is known as the "thesis defense" or "oral defense". It is a critical component of the evaluation process for graduate degrees. Graduate students' research ability cultivation, graduate degree assessment processes, criteria, supervision, purpose, problems and strategies are the key aspects typically covered in Chinese studies.

Zhang and Yuan (2017) found that there has been an improvement in the ability to apply research methods among English major graduate students, primarily reflected in the mastery of research tools. There has also been an enhancement in critical thinking skills and an increased awareness of problem-solving.

Xiong and Xu (2019) pointed out that improving the quality of graduate theses requires the collaboration and joint efforts of graduate students, mentors, training institutions, and graduate quality supervision departments. Each of these stakeholders plays a crucial role and cannot be neglected.

As for the graduate degree supervision, there are many related studies. For example, Li and Li (2023) conducted a survey analysis and found that the perceived level of stress among graduate students varied across different types of mentorship relationships. Graduate students in a mentorship relationship characterized by a supportive and beneficial bond experienced significantly lower levels of stress. In terms of mentor guidance behaviors, increasing the frequency of daily communication between mentors and students can reduce the perceived level of stress among graduate students.

In China, the challenges of promoting graduate students' research performance arise from societal factors. Certain existing regulations exacerbate the challenges encountered during graduate degree assessments. Furthermore, Gu and Chen (2011) investigated the present variations in supervision styles and identified some typical academic misconducts during graduate degree viva.

Ma, Lu and Zhao (2023) found that by implementing measures such as offering thesis writing courses, refining thesis templates, enforcing mentor selection and pre-defense systems, standardizing plagiarism detection and blind review systems, and improving the defense process, the quality of graduate theses can be effectively enhanced.

Dong (2021) believes that an important indicator of the quality of graduate education is the research and innovation ability of graduate students, which is primarily reflected in the quality of their master's theses. The study found that there are common issues in current graduate education, such as arbitrary topic selection, weak arguments, loose structure, imprecise language expression, and lack of innovation in research writing.

To improve the writing level of graduate students and enhance the quality of their theses, a pre-defense system before the formal viva is a favorable choice. Through the pre-defense, significant flaws in the research writing can be promptly identified, leveraging the guidance and wisdom of the mentor team to make timely corrections and significantly improve the quality of graduate theses.

1.5 Conceptual Framework

The conceptual framework is presented in Figure 1-1. The conceptual framework consists of some important building blocks. The theories included formative and summative assessment theory, intrinsic and extrinsic motivation theory, teacher-student relationship theory, and autonomy theory.

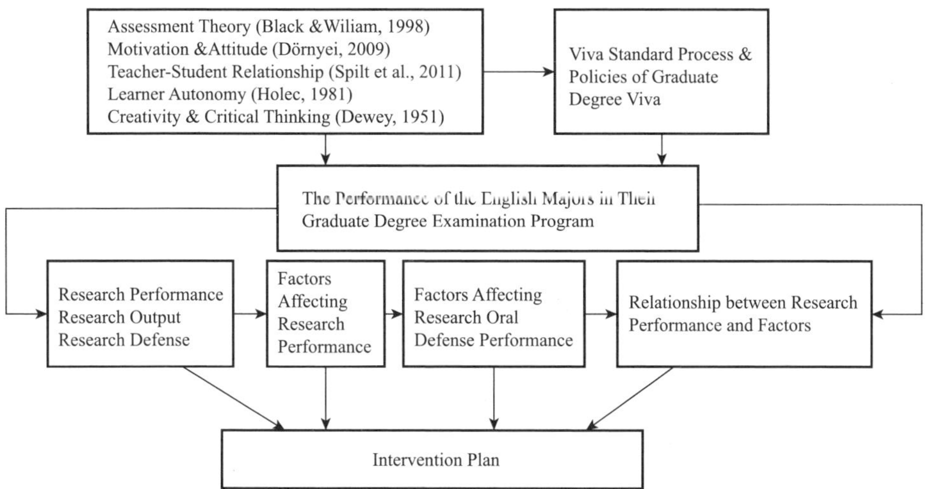

Figure 1-1 Conceptual Framework of the Study

1.6 Research Methodology

This part mainly describes the research methods used by the researchers in this study. It is divided into different parts, including research design, research environment, research respondents, research instruments, data collection procedures, and treatment of data.

1.7 Research Design

Research design refers to the overall strategy or plan that outlines how a research study was be conducted. It involved making decisions about various aspects of the study, such as the research questions, data collection methods, sample selection, and data analysis techniques.

This study utilized descriptive correlational research design. The research design involved the collection and analysis of both quantitative data and qualitative data, which were conducted separately. While the study is primarily qualitative in nature, it also included statistical descriptions. Data was gathered from instruments specifically designed for the target teachers and students, enabling a comprehensive understanding to answer the research questions.

1.8 Research Environment

The target participants of the study were the English major graduate degree teachers and students in Beijing, China's three representative universities. The survey research was conducted in Beijing. Codes like University A, University B, University C were used for confidentiality.

University A is a key university in China. The program was surveyed and its data was reported in the author's master degree dissertation. Their research achievements include literary criticism works and other translation works. There are 14 supervisors in its English major graduate program. Each year, it enrolls about 30 graduate students.

University B is a key university in Beijing. The program was surveyed and its data was reported in the author's master degree dissertation. Their research achievements include English education works and other translation works. There are 22 supervisors in its English major graduate program. Each year, it enrolls about 40 graduate students.

University C is a key university in China. The program was surveyed and its data would be reported. Their research achievements include bilingual dictionaries and other translation works. There are 12 supervisors in its English major graduate program. Each year, it enrolls about 10 graduate students.

1.9 Research Respondents or Participants

Before the author's study, an online searching of English major graduate degree programs in China was done. Through comparison, the three target programs were chosen as the sample due to their representativeness and the manageable principles. The exact number of participants can be seen in Table 1-1.

Table 1-1 Research Respondents

Participants	University A	University B	University C	Total
Teachers	10	10	10	30
Students	20	20	20	60
Total	30	30	30	90

For each university, a total of thirty participants were selected from the target program, consisting of ten supervisors and teachers who taught the graduate programs, along with twenty graduate students.

The chosen English major graduate degree teachers were both viva supervisors and examiners. They possess related knowledge and expertise in conducting vivas, comprehending the procedures and evaluation criteria involved. They also possess a heightened sensitivity towards this process. This research opportunity enables them to articulate and communicate their specialized insights and perspectives.

1.10 Research Instruments

Both quantitative and qualitative mixed methods were used in this study.

Quantitative method through the use of questionnaires collected numerical data and analyzed these using statistical treatments. On the other hand, qualitative research method collects non-numerical data. Qualitative method was employed in all the research questions to gather and analyze non-numerical data in order to gain deeper understanding and validate the quantitative data.

The research instruments were conducted in English because all participants were English major teachers and students who possessed a good understanding of the language. As suggested by Mckay (2008), it is essential to include a clear explanation of the research objectives at the start of the questionnaires and express appreciation to the participants at the end of the study. To enhance participant engagement and comprehension of the research purpose and theme, this study incorporated a concise introductory letter at the beginning of each questionnaire and expressed gratitude at the conclusion of the instruments.

According to Dörnyei (2010), the design of the research instrument should adhere to the principles of brevity and simplicity to prevent participant fatigue. Therefore, the author ensured that the instrument design was concise and straightforward, taking approximately 10 to 15 minutes for each participant to complete.

These researcher questionnaires and interview guides were based on *Several Opinions on Further Strictly Regulating the Quality Management of Academic Degrees and Graduate Education* issued by the Academic Degree Committee of the Chinese State Council and the Ministry of Education.

1.10.1 Quantitative

Questionnaire on the Research Performance of Graduate Students.

For Subproblem 1, a pre-survey was conducted to the graduate students and the oral examiners, listing at least 20 areas or common standards used in evaluating the students' research performance. Part I is the teachers' questionnaire that measured quantitatively the research performance of graduate students as to research output and research defense based on viva standards. Similar questionnaire was answered by the graduate students. Both questionnaires used a 5-point Likert scale where: 5=Outstanding; 4=Very Good; 3=Good; 2=Below Average; 1=Poor.

Questionnaire on Significant Factors Affecting Research Paper Output.

For Subproblem 2, a pre-survey was conducted to the graduate students and the oral examiners, listing at least 20 factors affecting students' performance in writing the research paper as basis in crafting the questionnaire. This is Part II-A in the teachers' questionnaire, as well as in the students' questionnaire. A 5-point Likert scale was used where: 1=never or hardly ever, 2=seldom, 3=sometimes, 4=frequently, 5=always.

Factors affecting the oral defense based on viva standards measures Subproblem 3 and from the results of the pre-survey from the graduate students and the oral examiners, a questionnaire was constructed to measure quantitatively these factors. While Part II-A measured the research output of graduate students, Part II-B determined the factors affecting graduate students' oral defense via viva using the 5-point Likert scale as in SOP#3.

Subproblem 4 answered the relationship between the research performance of the students and the identified factors by themselves and the oral examiners. Using Spearman coefficient correlation, the data from teachers' survey and students' survey for Subproblem 2 and Subproblem 3 were analyzed to get the relationship between the two variables.

1.10.2 Qualitative

Follow-up interview questions were designed by the researcher after the questionnaire data was collected and analyzed. The questions focused more on participants' prevalent attitudes, beliefs and opinions about viva standards. They were used to answer all the five research questions.

1.10.3 Reliability and Validity Tests

In line with Mckay's (2008) suggestion, the author recognized the importance of piloting and revising the instrument to ensure internal consistency. Prior to implementing it in the three target programs, the author conducted a pilot study with other individuals to enhance the validity of the research. Instruments were validated by 3 instrument experts (2 from the overseas and 1 from China). The validation is in terms of "Face Validity" and "Content Validity". Validation was obtained first before the use of the instruments in gathering the data.

To ensure the validity and reliability of the research, it is crucial to carefully select the sample (Wagner, 2010). In this study, the three specific programs at the case universities in Beijing were chosen as they are representative and manageable in terms of sample size. This selection process enhances the credibility and dependability of the research findings.

The instruments were reviewed and validated by 3 instrument experts (2 from the overseas and 1 from China). The validation was in terms of "Face Validity" and "Content Validity". Validation was obtained first before the use of the instruments in gathering the data. Then proceed to Cronbach' Validity and Reliability Test. After the instrument turned out to be valid and reliable the researcher administered it to the respondents. The Cronbach reliability was computed by a statistician. Table 1-2 shows Cronbach's alpha reliability test result of student questionnaire. Table 1-3 shows Cronbach's alpha reliability test result of teacher questionnaire.

Table 1-2 Cronbach's Alpha Reliability Test Result of Student Questionnaire

Cronbach' s Alpha	Number of items
.970	45

From Table 1-2, it can be seen that the reliability coefficient value is 0.970, which is greater than 0.9, indicating that the student questionnaire has high reliability quality and can be used for further use.

Table1-3 Cronbach's Alpha Reliability Test Result of Teacher Questionnaire

Cronbach' s Alpha	Number of items
.948	45

From Table 1-3, it can be seen that the reliability coefficient value is 0.948, which is greater than 0.9, indicating that the student questionnaire has high reliability quality and can also be used for further use.

Furthermore, the data analysis phase played a crucial role in establishing the reliability and validity of the study. According to Maxwell (2005), biases and errors in the interpretation of qualitative data could potentially lead to misinterpretations by the researcher. To prevent this issue, the researcher sought assistance from their supervisor, who critically examined and evaluated the interpretation of the qualitative data. Subsequently, the suggestions provided by the supervisor were taken into consideration, leading to necessary revisions and re-interpretations of the data.

Regarding the statistical data analysis, the researcher used straightforward yet reliable statistical methods, to enhance the validity and reliability of the study. Additionally, in order to minimize errors, the data statistics were reviewed by two colleagues who were familiar with the subject matter.

1.11 Data Collection Procedure

The collection of data was done in a chorological manner which consist of three phases.

Phase 1: Preparation. The researcher approached these three universities' English major graduate degree programs' directors via emails, and sent them teachers' and students' participant information statement, questionnaires and interview guide. The directors helped publish the research information and passed the questionnaires to the participants of this research.

Phase 2: Implementation. The data was collected within one month. As discussed above, the initial contact with the three target programs' directors was conducted. It is important to make participants welcome the study (Wagner, 2010), so the researcher explained the research purpose and appreciated their cooperation. After getting the participants' permission and the ethic approval, the questionnaires were conducted online or face to face. The interviews were conducted online. In the questionnaire for teachers and students, both qualitative data and statistical data were collected. Qualitative data were collected from interviews. The complete set of data, which showed supervision, implementation and assessment in the target programs and the participants' beliefs towards the assessment, reflected its influence to promote China's English major graduate degree students' research performance to a certain extent.

Phase 3: Analysis and reporting. Interviews were conducted to support and validate the quantitative data of Subproblems 1 and 2. All these quantitative and qualitative data were analyzed which were made as basis in designing an innovative action plan. Conclusion was drawn and recommendations were offered to complete the research process.

1.12 Treatment of Data

To answer the different research problems, the following research instruments were constructed in gathering the data that were needed in the study.

1.12.1 Quantitative

A pre-survey was conducted to the graduate students and the oral examiners, listing at least 20 areas or common standards used in evaluating the students' research performance. To answer Subproblem 1, a questionnaire was crafted to assess the research performance of English major graduate students on research output (Part 1A) which includes topic selection, academic value, updated theories, appropriate research method, analysis skills, scientific conclusion, doable recommendations and writing format. Part 1B was on research defense based on viva standards with indicators on answering viewpoint, language expression ability, mastering basic knowledge, independent research ability. This questionnaire was answered by both teachers and graduate students. The instrument adopted a 5-point Likert scale. Both questionnaires used a 5-point Likert scale where: 5=Outstanding; 4=Very Good; 3=Good; 2=Below Average; 1=Poor. Mean and standard deviation were used to treat the data.

This was Part 2A of the constructed questionnaire in answer to Subproblem 2. A pre-survey was conducted to the graduate students and the oral examiners, listing at least 20 factors affecting students' performance in writing the research paper as basis in crafting the questionnaire. With identified factors, viz: willingness to improve the research, guidance of the supervisor, research experience, literature reading quantity, and language writing ability.

Part 2B of the questionnaire measured the factors affecting the oral defense of graduate students using viva standards (Subproblem 3) which include preparation, emotional management, research level of the paper and language and defense ability. A 5-point Likert scale was used: 5=always, 4=frequently, 3=sometimes, 2=seldom, 1=never. Part 2A and Part 2B were answered by graduate students (who defended) and panel members. The statistical treatment used was mean and standard deviation.

Subproblem 4 answered the relationship between the research performance of the students and the identified factors by themselves and the oral examiners. The data from teachers' questionnaires and students' questionnaires for Subproblem 2 and Subproblem 3 were compared to get the relationship between the two quantitative variables using Spearman rho correlation coefficient.

1.12.2 Qualitative

Follow-up interview questions were designed by the researcher after the questionnaire data was collected and analyzed. The questions focused more on participants' prevalent attitudes, beliefs and opinions about viva standards. They were used to answer all the five research questions.

The collected data is subjected to interpretive analysis, which involves examining both the statistical and qualitative data. The statistical data includes Mean, Standard Deviation, and other relevant statistical measures to understand the distribution and patterns of responses. The qualitative data, on the other hand, provides more detailed and descriptive information about the participants perceptions and experiences related to the different dimensions of the graduate degree program.

1.13 Ethical Considerations

Ethical considerations were an essential component of the data analysis procedure. They ensured that the rights and well-being of individuals or groups involved in the data collection or analysis process were respected and protected. Researcher obtained informed consent from individuals or groups participating in the data collection process. Participants were fully aware of the purpose of the research, how their data would be collected and analyzed, and any potential risks or benefits.

Data was collected and analyzed in a way that protected the privacy and confidentiality of participants. This included ensuring that personal identifying information was anonymized or de-identified and stored securely. Researcher clarified who owned the data collected and how it would be shared and used. It was important to obtain permission from participants before sharing or using their data for purposes beyond the original research scope.

Researcher took steps to minimize any potential harm or negative consequences that might arise from data analysis. This included ensuring that data was handled and analyzed in a way that respected cultural norms and values and did not cause harm to individuals or groups. Researcher strived to maintain the integrity and accuracy of the data throughout the analysis process. This included documenting any data cleaning or transformation procedures and being transparent about any limitations or biases that might impact the analysis.

The data processing of this study strictly followed the principle of confidentiality. The respondents appeared in the form of code. All kinds of materials were properly kept by the researcher. After the respondents' consent, they were used for the design of the paper and would not be provided to a third party. After data processing, it was only limited to the analysis of the questions raised, and no judgment was made on the right or wrong policies of the relevant universities. By considering these ethical considerations throughout the data analysis process, researcher could ensure that the research was conducted ethically and with the utmost respect for the rights and well-being of participants.

Chapter 2
Research Performance of the Graduate Students in Research Output and Research Defense

2.1 Introduction

In this chapter, the focus is on reporting the data collected from the Part I of the questionnaires and interviews administered to both teachers and students in the three target English major graduate degree programs. The data pertains to the different dimensions of the graduate degree program for English majors and their levels of performancc. Thc aim is to gain insights into the participants' perceptions of the program' s performance in each dimension and to identify any patterns or trends that may exist. It answers SOP 1.

The collected data is subjected to interpretive analysis, which involves examining both the statistical and qualitative data. The statistical data includes Mean, Standard Deviation, and other relevant statistical measures to understand the distribution and patterns of responses. The qualitative data, on the other hand, provides more detailed and descriptive information about the participants perceptions and experiences related to the different dimensions of the graduate degree program, which was organized by themes.

The research used the questionnaire survey method to analyze the level of performance of English majors' graduate degree program from two perspectives: research paper output and research defense based on viva standards. Teachers and students had similar answers based on the current assessment policies. Therefore, they used the same questionnaire which measured the level of performance of English majors' graduate degree program. They read each statement and rate each using a 5-point Likert scale where: 5=Outstanding; 4=Very Good; 3=Good; 2=Below Average; 1=Poor.

The questionnairc includcs cight broad questions for research paper output: 1) Thesis topic selection, 2) Academic values, 3) Updated theories, 4) Appropriate research methods, 5) Analysis skills, 6) Scientific conclusion, 7) Realistic recommendations, and 8) Writing format. The questionnaire includes five broad questions for research defense based on viva standards: 1) Answering viewpoint, 2) Language Expression Ability, 3) Mastering basic knowledge, and 4) Independent research ability.

2.2 Research Paper Output

2.2.1 Thesis Topic Selection

Table 2-1 Thesis Topic Selection (N=90)

Items	The research topic is selected based on an existing problem		The research topic is original and interesting	
University A teacher (N=10)	M	4.40	M	4.40
	SD	0.843	SD	0.843
	Interpretation	Very High	Interpretation	Very High
University A student (N=20)	M	4.35	M	4.30
	SD	0.671	SD	0.865
	Interpretation	Very High	Interpretation	Very High

(*to be continued*)

Items	The research topic is selected based on an existing problem		The research topic is original and interesting	
University B teacher (N=10)	M	4.50	M	4.40
	SD	0.527	SD	0.699
	Interpretation	Very High	Interpretation	Very High
University B student (N=20)	M	3.50	M	3.40
	SD	0.607	SD	0.503
	Interpretation	High	Interpretation	High
University C teacher (N=10)	M	4.10	M	4.10
	SD	0.568	SD	0.568
	Interpretation	High	Interpretation	High
University C student (N=20)	M	4.20	M	4.50
	SD	0.834	SD	0.607
	Interpretation	Very High	Interpretation	Very High
TOTAL (N=90)	M	4.12	M	4.14
	SD	0.762	SD	0.787
	Interpretation	High	Interpretation	High

Legend: 4.21–5.00, Very High; 3.41–4.20, High; 2.61–3.40, Moderate; 1.81–2.60, Low; 1.00–1.80, Poor.

Thesis topic selection ranked high as shown in Table 2-1. Both teachers and students believed "research topic is selected based on an existing problem" and "research topic is original and interesting" were very important criteria to assess students' research paper output. Therefore, they were asked in the questionnaire. Table 2-1 shows the Mean and Standard Deviation of the data from teachers and students in the three target programs.

Based on the total data from all universities combined, the mean rating for the criterion "The research topic is selected based on an existing problem" is 4.12, with a standard deviation of 0.762. The mean rating for the criterion "The research topic is original and interesting" is 4.14, with a standard deviation of 0.787. Both means fall within the "High" interpretation category for both criteria. This indicates that overall, the research topic is rated highly in terms of being based on an existing problem and being original and interesting by the participants across all universities.

According to the data as rated by University A teachers, the mean rating for the criterion "The research topic is selected based on an existing problem" is 4.4, with a standard deviation of 0.843. The mean rating for the criterion "The research topic is original and interesting" is also 4.4, with a standard deviation of 0.843. Both means fall within the "Very High" interpretation category for both criteria. This indicates that University A teachers have rated the research topic as being based on an existing problem and as being original and interesting very highly.

Based on the data as rated by students of University A, the mean rating for the criterion "The research topic is selected based on an existing problem" is 4.35, with a standard deviation of 0.671. The mean rating for the criterion "The research topic is original and interesting" is 4.3, with a standard deviation of 0.865. Both means fall within the "Very High" interpretation category for both criteria. This indicates that University A students have also rated the research topic as being based on an existing problem and as being original and interesting very highly, similar to University A teachers.

Based on the table, the mean rating from University B teachers for the criterion "The research topic is selected based on an existing problem" is 4.5, with a standard deviation of 0.527. The mean rating for the criterion "The research topic is original and interesting" is 4.4, with a standard deviation of 0.699. Both means fall within the "Very High" interpretation category for both criteria. This indicates that University B teachers have rated the research topic highly in terms of being based on an existing problem and being original and interesting.

As rated by the students of University B, the mean rating for the criterion "The research topic is selected based on an existing problem" is 3.5, with a standard deviation of 0.607. The mean rating for the criterion "The research topic is original and interesting" is 3.4, with a standard deviation of 0.503. Both means fall within the "High" interpretation category for both criteria. This indicates that University B students have rated the research topic as being based on an existing problem and as being original and interesting at a high level, but not as highly as University A students and teachers.

The data of University C teachers reveals that the mean rating for the criterion "The research topic is selected based on an existing problem" is 4.1, with a standard deviation of 0.568. The mean rating for the criterion "The research topic is original and interesting" is 4.1, with a standard deviation of 0.568. Both means fall within the "High" interpretation category for both criteria. This indicates that University C teachers have rated the research topic as being based on an existing problem and as being original and interesting at a high level, similar to University B students but not as high as University B teachers.

The data of University C students shows that, the mean rating for the criterion "The research topic is selected based on an existing problem" is 4.2, with a standard deviation of 0.834. The mean rating for the criterion "The research topic is original and interesting" is 4.5, with a standard deviation of 0.607. Both means fall within the "Very High" interpretation category for both criteria. This indicates that University C students have rated the research topic very highly in terms of being based on an existing problem and being original and interesting, surpassing the ratings of both University A and University B students and teachers.

The data suggests that a high rating of a research topic could indicate its perceived innovativeness, engagement, and thought-provoking nature among participants. This interpretation aligns with existing literature on motivation and topic selection in research. Dörnyei and Ushioda (2009) extensively discussed the importance of motivation in promoting learning. They argued that motivation is crucial for sustaining engagement and effort in academic tasks. When students are intrinsically motivated by a research topic, they are more likely to demonstrate enthusiasm, curiosity, and a willingness to invest effort into their work. This is because they find the topic inherently interesting and relevant to their personal interests or goals. Murray, Gao, and Lamb (2011) also highlighted the significance of intrinsic motivation over extrinsic motivation in academic contexts. Intrinsic motivation refers to engaging in an activity for its inherent satisfaction or enjoyment, while extrinsic motivation involves external rewards or pressures. They argued that fostering intrinsic motivation leads to better outcomes and reduces the psychological pressure that may arise from solely relying on extrinsic motivators.

Therefore, when graduate students are allowed to select research topics that align with their interests, passions, and intrinsic motivations, they are more likely to be engaged and committed to their research endeavors. This reduces the likelihood of feeling overwhelmed by external pressures and enhances their overall learning experience. The analysis implies that graduate degree programs with lower ratings may need to reconsider their approach to supervising students' research topic selection. By providing guidance and support in selecting topics that resonate with students' intrinsic motivations, these programs can potentially improve student engagement and research outcomes. Overall, the assertion that a high rating of a research topic can drive engagement, generate new insights, and lead to impactful research outcomes is supported by the existing literature on motivation and topic selection in academic contexts.

2.2.2 Academic Values

Academic values ranked secondly high as shown in Table 2-2, which was emphasized in *Notice on Further Tightening the Administration of Doctoral Dissertation Defense*. Both teachers and students believed "research has theoretical values" and "research has application values" were very important criteria to assess students' research paper output. Therefore, they were made into the questionnaire. Table 2-2 shows the Mean and Standard Deviation of the data from teachers and students in the three target programs.

Table 2-2 Academic Values (N=90)

Items	The research has theoretical values		The research has application values	
University A teacher (N=10)	M	4.40	M	4.20
	SD	0.966	SD	1.317
	Interpretation	Very High	Interpretation	High
University A student (N=20)	M	4.05	M	3.55
	SD	0.759	SD	1.099
	Interpretation	High	Interpretation	Moderate
University B teacher (N=10)	M	4.10	M	4.30
	SD	0.738	SD	0.675
	Interpretation	High	Interpretation	Very High
University B student (N=20)	M	3.35	M	3.35
	SD	0.489	SD	0.489
	Interpretation	Moderate	Interpretation	Moderate

(*to be continued*)

Items	The research has theoretical values		The research has application values	
University C teacher (N=10)	M	3.60	M	4.20
	SD	0.843	SD	0.632
	Interpretation	High	Interpretation	High
University C student (N=20)	M	4.25	M	4.45
	SD	0.851	SD	0.759
	Interpretation	Very High	Interpretation	Very High
TOTAL (N=90)	M	3.93	M	3.93
	SD	0.832	SD	0.946
	Interpretation	High	Interpretation	High

Legend: 4.21–5.00, Very High; 3.41–4.20, High; 2.61–3.40, Moderate; 1.81–2.60, Low; 1.00–1.80, Poor.

Based on the overall data for all teachers and students, the mean rating for the item "The research has theoretical values" is 3.93 with a standard deviation of 0.832. This indicates that, on average, the participants perceive the research to have a high level of theoretical value. The mean rating for the item "The research has application values" is 3.93 with a standard deviation of 0.946. This suggests that, on average, the participants perceive the research to have a high level of application value as well. Therefore, the overall interpretation of the data indicates that both teachers and students collectively rated the research highly in terms of both theoretical and application values. This suggests that there is a general consensus among the participants that the research has strong theoretical foundations and practical applications, with a high emphasis on both aspects. However, there are some moderate ratings.

Based on the data provided, the mean rating for the item "The research has theoretical values" is 4.4 with a standard deviation of 0.966. This indicates that, on the average, University A teachers perceived the research to have a very high level of theoretical value. The mean rating for the item "The research has application values" is 4.2 with a standard deviation of 1.317. This suggests that, on average, University A teachers perceive the research to have a high level of application value. Therefore, University A teachers rated the research highly in both theoretical and application values. The interpretation of the data indicates that they consider the research to have strong theoretical foundations and practical implications.

For University A, the mean rating of students for the item "The research has theoretical values" is 4.05 with a standard deviation of 0.759. This indicates that, on the average, University A students perceive the research to have a high level of theoretical value. The mean rating for the item "The research has application values" is 3.55 with a standard deviation of 1.099. This suggests that, on average, University A students perceive the research to have a moderate level of application value. Therefore, University A students rated the research highly in terms of theoretical value and moderately in terms of application value. The interpretation of the data indicates that they consider the research to have strong theoretical foundations, but they may see room for improvement in its practical applications.

For University B, the mean rating for the item "The research has theoretical values" is 4.1 with a standard deviation of 0.738. This indicates that, on the average, University B teachers perceive the research to have a high level of theoretical value. The mean rating for the item "The research has application values" is 4.3 with a standard deviation of 0.675. This suggests that, on average, University B teachers perceive the research to have a very high level of application value. Therefore, University B teachers rated the research highly in both theoretical and application values. The interpretation of the data indicates that they consider the research to have strong theoretical foundations and practical applications, with a particularly high emphasis on its application values.

The data from University B as rated by the students shows that the mean rating for the item "The research has theoretical values" is 3.35 with a standard deviation of 0.489. This indicates that, on the average, University B students perceive the research to have a moderate level of theoretical value. The mean rating for the item "The research has application values" is 3.35 with a standard deviation of 0.489. This suggests that, on average, University B students perceive the research to have a moderate level of application value. Therefore, University B students rated the research equally in terms of both theoretical and application values, with a moderate perception for both aspects. The interpretation of the data indicates that they consider the research to have some theoretical and practical value, but there might be room for improvement in both areas.

According to the data of University C, the mean rating for the item "The research has theoretical values" is 3.6 with a standard deviation of 0.843. This indicates that, on the average, University C teachers perceive the research to have a high level of theoretical value. The mean rating for the item "The research has application values" is 4.2 with a standard deviation of 0.632. This suggests that, on average, University C teachers perceive the research to have a high level of application value. Therefore, University C teachers rated the research highly in both theoretical and application values. The interpretation of the data indicates that they consider the research to have strong theoretical foundations and practical applications, with a high emphasis on both aspects.

Based on the data provided, the mean rating for the item "The research has theoretical values" is 4.25 with a standard deviation of 0.851. This indicates that, on average, University C students perceive the research to have a very high level of theoretical value. The mean rating for the item "The research has application values" is 4.45 with a standard deviation of 0.759. This suggests that, on average, University C students perceive the research to have a very high level of application value. Therefore, University C students rated the research very highly in terms of both theoretical and application values. The interpretation of the data indicates that they consider the research to have exceptionally strong theoretical foundations and practical applications, with a very high emphasis on both aspects. This indicates that University C students highly appreciate the theoretical and practical value of the research.

Both teachers and students at University A rated the research highly in terms of theoretical values, with teachers giving it a "Very High" interpretation and students rating it as "High." In terms of application values, teachers rated it as "High" while students rated it as "Moderate." Teachers at University B rated the research highly in both theoretical and application values, with application values rated as "Very High". However, students at University B rated the research at a moderate level for both theoretical and application values. Teachers at University C rated the research highly in terms of application values, with students rating it as "Very High". For theoretical values, teachers and students at University C rated the research as "High" and "Very High", respectively.

Overall, the data shows that the perception of theoretical and application values of the research varies across different groups. University C students rated the research highest in both theoretical and application values, while University B students rated it the lowest. The total ratings indicate a moderate to high level of perceived theoretical and application values across all respondents. It is important to consider these variations in interpretation when assessing the perceived values of the research topic across different groups.

It is crucial to support and promote research activities among English major graduate students to maximize these benefits, increase the theoretical and application values of the graduate degree research. Li (2023) believed strengthening the academic research and practical exploration of graduate academic values and improving the effectiveness of leadership were key measures to promote the high-quality development of graduate education. This belief in the importance of strengthening academic research, practical exploration, and leadership effectiveness in promoting high-quality development in graduate education is supported by the existing literature on graduate education and research. These measures are essential for enhancing the academic value of graduate research, advancing knowledge, fostering professional development, and promoting career opportunities and personal fulfillment among graduate students in English majors. Therefore, enhancing the academic value of English major graduate research is essential for the advancement of knowledge, professional development, academic reputation, career opportunities, and personal fulfillment of individuals in the field.

2.2.3 Updated Theories

Updated theories ranked thirdly high as shown in Table 2-3 below which was also emphasized in *Notice on Further Tightening the Administration of Doctoral Dissertation Defense*. Both teachers and students believed "theories are relevant and illuminating to the research" and "theories are fully and clearly presented in the research" were very important criteria to assess students' research paper output. Therefore, they were made into the questionnaire. Table 2-3 shows the Mean and Standard Deviation of the data from teachers and students in the three target programs.

Table 2-3 Updated Theories (N=90)

Items	The theories are relevant and illuminating to the research		The theories are fully and clearly presented in the research	
University A teacher (N=10)	M	4.40	M	4.40
	SD	0.966	SD	0.699
	Interpretation	Very High	Interpretation	Very High

(*to be continued*)

Items	The theories are relevant and illuminating to the research		The theories are fully and clearly presented in the research	
University A student (N=20)	M	4.25	M	4.00
	SD	0.786	SD	0.858
	Interpretation	Very High	Interpretation	High
University B teacher (N=10)	M	4.30	M	4.50
	SD	0.675	SD	0.527
	Interpretation	Very High	Interpretation	Very High
University B student (N=20)	M	3.45	M	3.45
	SD	0.510	SD	0.510
	Interpretation	High	Interpretation	High
University C teacher (N=10)	M	3.90	M	4.00
	SD	0.568	SD	0.667
	Interpretation	High	Interpretation	High
University C student (N=20)	M	4.40	M	4.30
	SD	0.681	SD	0.733
	Interpretation	Very High	Interpretation	Very High
TOTAL (N=90)	M	4.09	M	4.04
	SD	0.774	SD	0.763
	Interpretation	High	Interpretation	High

Legend: 4.21–5.00, Very High; 3.41–4.20, High; 2.61–3.40, Moderate; 1.81–2.60, Low; 1.00–1.80, Poor.

Based on the updated data for the total scores across all universities and participants, the mean ratings for the relevance and illumination of theories are 4.09 and for the full and clear presentation of theories are 4.04. The standard deviations for these two criteria are 0.774 and 0.763, respectively. The interpretation for both criteria based on these updated total scores is still considered "High". This suggests that overall, the participants across the universities rated the relevance, illumination, and presentation of theories in research as high. Nevertheless, discrepancies arise not only between various programs but also between educators and students.

The data from 20 students of University A illustrates that the mean rating for the criterion "The theories are relevant and illuminating to the research" is 4.4, with a standard deviation of 0.966. The mean rating for the criterion "The theories are fully and clearly presented in the research" is also 4.4, with a standard deviation of 0.699. Both means fall within the "Very High" interpretation category for both criteria. This data suggests that University A's teachers believe students excel in both the relevance and presentation of theories in their research, with high mean scores and relatively low standard deviations, indicating consistency and high performance in these areas.

According to the data of University A, there are a total of 20 valid students responses for the two statements. This data indicates that University A's students perceive theories as highly relevant and illuminating to research, with a mean score of 4.25 and a very low standard deviation of 0.786. However, their perception of the presentation of theories in research is slightly lower with a mean score of 4.00 and a higher standard deviation of 0.858, though still considered high. This suggests that while students acknowledge the importance of theories in research, there may be some variability in the clarity and completeness of how theories are presented in their work.

As rated by 10 teachers of University B, the data indicates that the perception of theories being relevant and illuminating to research is very high, with a mean score of 4.3 and a standard deviation of 0.675. The perception of theories being fully and clearly presented in research is also very high, with a mean score of 4.5 and a lower standard deviation of 0.527. This suggests that the teachers at University B consider theories as highly relevant and illuminating to research, and also perceive that these theories are presented in a fully and clearly manner within the research.

The data from University B indicates that for University B's students, the perception of theories being relevant and illuminating to research is high, with a mean score of 3.45 and a standard deviation of 0.510. The perception of theories being fully and clearly presented in research is also high, with a mean score of 3.45 and a standard deviation of 0.510. This suggests that students at University B perceive theories as being important and insightful to research, and they also believe that these theories are presented in a clear and comprehensive manner within the research they encounter.

The data indicates that for University C's teachers, the perception of theories being relevant and illuminating to research is high, with a mean score of 3.9 and a standard deviation of 0.568. The perception of theories being fully and clearly presented in research is also high, with a mean score of 4.0 and a standard deviation of 0.667. This suggests that the teachers at University C consider theories as highly relevant and illuminating to research, and also perceive that these theories are presented in a fully and clearly manner within the research. The slightly higher mean score for the presentation of theories compared to the relevance indicates a strong emphasis on the clarity and thoroughness of presenting theories in research at University C.

The data indicates that for University C's students, the perception of theories being relevant and illuminating to research is very high, with a mean score of 4.4 and a standard deviation of 0.681. The perception of theories being fully and clearly presented in research is also very high, with a mean score of 4.3 and a standard deviation of 0.733. This suggests that students at University C highly value the relevance and illuminating aspects of theories in research and perceive that these theories are presented in a very clear and comprehensive manner within the research they encounter. The high mean scores and low standard deviations indicate a strong consensus among the students at University C regarding the importance and presentation of theories in research.

The data provided in the summary highlights the perspectives of both teachers and students from three different universities on the relevance, illumination, and presentation of theories in research. However, there were variations in ratings among different universities and between teachers and students within the same university.

There were differences in ratings among the three universities, both in terms of the mean scores and the interpretations of the ratings. For example, University B students rated the relevance and illumination of theories lower compared to other universities, while University C students rated the presentation of theories slightly lower than the other universities. In general, teachers tended to rate the theories as more relevant, illuminating, and well-presented compared to students. Teachers consistently rated the theories as more relevant, illuminating, and well-presented compared to students across all universities. This could be attributed to the teachers' expertise and experience in the subject matter, leading them to have a deeper understanding and appreciation of the theories presented. Students have varying levels of familiarity with the theories (Bakhshi, Weisi & Yousofi, 2022), which could influence their perception of the relevance, illumination, and presentation of the theories in the research.

By considering these factors, we can better understand how students' familiarity with theories influences their perception of research relevance, illumination, and presentation. When students encounter theories they are already familiar with, they may find it easier to understand and engage with the material. Conversely, encountering unfamiliar theories may lead to confusion or difficulty in grasping the concepts presented. Some students may thrive when presented with challenging or unfamiliar theories, finding them intellectually stimulating, while others may struggle or disengage if the material exceeds their current level of understanding. Students with well-developed schemas related to certain theories may more readily integrate new information into their existing knowledge structures, facilitating comprehension and retention.

The high ratings for the relevance, illumination, and presentation of theories in the research suggest that the research successfully incorporated theories that were well-received by participants from different universities. The discrepancies in ratings between teachers and students, as well as among different universities, highlight the importance of considering diverse perspectives and feedback when evaluating the effectiveness of theories in research.

2.2.4 Appropriate Research Methods

Appropriate research methods ranked thirdly high as shown in the table below, which was emphasized in both *Notice on Further Tightening the Administration of Doctoral Dissertation Defense* and *The Viva Standard Process and Policies of Graduate Degree Viva*. Both teachers and students believed "research methods are scientific and advanced" and "research methods are suitably adopted" were very important criteria to assess students' research paper output. Therefore, they were made into the questionnaire. Table 2-4 shows the Mean and Standard Deviation of the data from teachers and students in the three target programs.

Table 2-4 Appropriate Research Methods (N=90)

Items	The research methods are scientific and advanced		The research methods are suitably adopted	
University A teacher (N=10)	M	4.30	M	4.40
	SD	0.823	SD	0.843
	Interpretation	Very High	Interpretation	Very High

(*to be continued*)

Items	The research methods are scientific and advanced		The research methods are suitably adopted	
University A student (N=20)	M	3.80	M	4.15
	SD	1.240	SD	0.875
	Interpretation	High	Interpretation	High
University B teacher (N=10)	M	4.20	M	4.40
	SD	0.789	SD	0.699
	Interpretation	Very High	Interpretation	Very High
University B student (N=20)	M	3.40	M	3.45
	SD	0.503	SD	0.510
	Interpretation	Moderate	Interpretation	High
University C teacher (N=10)	M	4.00	M	4.10
	SD	0.816	SD	0.568
	Interpretation	High	Interpretation	High
University C student (N=20)	M	4.40	M	4.45
	SD	0.754	SD	0.686
	Interpretation	Very High	Interpretation	Very High
TOTAL (N=90)	M	3.97	M	4.11
	SD	0.917	SD	0.785
	Interpretation	High	Interpretation	High

Legend: 4.21–5.00, Very High; 3.41–4.20, High; 2.61–3.40, Moderate; 1.81–2.60, Low; 1.00–1.80, Poor.

For the total data from all three universities, the mean ratings for the research methods are 3.97 for being scientific and advanced, and 4.11 for being suitably adopted. The standard deviations are 0.917 and 0.785 respectively. The interpretation suggests a high level of agreement and consistency among all participants (teachers and students from all three universities) in their evaluation of the research methods.

The mean ratings indicate that the participants generally viewed the research methods as being both scientifically rigorous and advanced, as well as suitably adopted. The low standard deviations suggest that the ratings were relatively consistent across the different participants, further indicating a strong level of agreement in their assessment of the research methods.

The research methods used by University A teachers received high ratings for being both scientific and advanced (Mean=4.30, SD=0.823) as well as suitably adopted (Mean=4.40, SD=0.843), with a very high level of agreement and consistency among the participants.

The data from University A students indicate that they rated the research methods slightly lower than the teachers, with a mean score of 3.80 for being scientific and advanced and 4.15 for being suitably adopted. The standard deviations are 1.240 and 0.875 respectively. Despite the slight difference in ratings, the interpretation still suggests a high level of agreement and consistency among the students in evaluating the research methods.

The data from University B teachers show that they rated the research methods highly for being scientific and advanced (Mean=4.20, SD=0.789) and suitably adopted (Mean=4.40, SD=0.699). The interpretation of these results indicates a very high level of agreement and consistency among the teachers in their evaluation of the research methods at University B.

The data from University B students indicate that they rated the research methods lower than the teachers, with a mean score of 3.40 for being scientific and advanced and 3.45 for being suitably adopted. The standard deviations are 0.503 and 0.510 respectively. The interpretation suggests a moderate level of agreement among the students for the scientific and advanced aspect, and a high level of agreement for the suitability adoption aspect in their evaluation of the research methods at University B.

The data from University C teachers show that they rated the research methods highly for being scientific and advanced (Mean=4.00, SD=0.816) and suitably adopted (Mean=4.10, SD=0.568). The interpretation of these results indicates a high level of agreement and consistency among the teachers in their evaluation of the research methods at University C.

The data from University C students indicate that they rated the research methods highly, with a mean score of 4.40 for being scientific and advanced and 4.45 for being suitably adopted. The standard deviations are 0.754 and 0.686 respectively. The interpretation suggests a very high level of agreement and consistency among the students in their evaluation of the research methods at University C.

In comparing the mean ratings for the research methods between the two criteria ("scientific and advanced" and "suitably adopted"), we can see that the participants rate the methods slightly higher in terms of being suitably adopted (mean rating of 4.11) compared to being scientific and advanced (mean rating of 3.97). This suggests that the participants have perceived the research methods as more practically applicable and relevant to their needs rather than solely focusing on their theoretical sophistication.

Xu (2020) emphasized on the importance of research methods in writing academic papers. This emphasis on the importance of research methods in academic writing aligns with the established principles of rigorous research methodology, credibility, reproducibility, and critical thinking in scholarly inquiry. Research methods are crucial for ensuring the rigor and validity of academic papers. Transparent and well-documented research methods facilitate the reproducibility of research findings, allowing other researchers to replicate the study and verify its results. A strong emphasis on research methods enhances the credibility of academic papers. Research methods play a crucial role in guiding the design of academic papers. Engaging with research methods promotes critical thinking skills among researchers.

The low standard deviations for both criteria indicate that there was a high level of agreement and consistency among the participants in their evaluations. This consistency suggests that the participants from all three universities, including both teachers and students, shared similar perspectives on the effectiveness and quality of the research methods being used.

Overall, the data indicates that there is a strong consensus among the participants regarding the positive evaluation of the research methods, highlighting their perceived value and effectiveness in the academic setting.

2.2.5 Analysis Skills

Table 2-5 shows that Analysis skills ranked high. Both teachers and students believed "presenting unique insights into data" and "using the conjoint analysis of macro and micro" were very important criteria to assess students' research paper output. Thus, the two statements were asked in the questionnaire. Table 2-5 shows the Mean and Standard Deviation of the data from teachers and students in the three target programs.

Table 2-5 Analysis Skills (N=90)

Items	Presenting unique insights into data		Using the conjoint analysis of macro and micro	
University A teacher (N=10)	M	4.20	M	3.50
	SD	1.229	SD	1.179
	Interpretation	High	Interpretation	High
University A student (N=20)	M	4.10	M	4.20
	SD	0.852	SD	0.696
	Interpretation	High	Interpretation	High
University B teacher (N=10)	M	3.90	M	3.90
	SD	0.738	SD	0.876
	Interpretation	High	Interpretation	High
University B student (N=20)	M	3.45	M	3.45
	SD	0.605	SD	0.605
	Interpretation	High	Interpretation	High
University C teacher (N=10)	M	4.00	M	3.90
	SD	0.667	SD	0.876
	Interpretation	High	Interpretation	High
University C student (N=20)	M	4.30	M	4.20
	SD	0.801	SD	0.768
	Interpretation	Very High	Interpretation	High
TOTAL (N=90)	M	3.98	M	3.89
	SD	0.848	SD	0.841
	Interpretation	High	Interpretation	High

Legend: 4.21–5.00, Very High; 3.41–4.20, High; 2.61–3.40, Moderate; 1.81–2.60, Low; 1.00–1.80, Poor.

Based on the total data for the three programs, which includes all students and teachers, the overall mean rating for the first set of data is 3.98, indicating a high level of satisfaction among both students and teachers. The standard deviation for the mean rating is 0.848, suggesting moderate variability in the ratings among the total population. The mean rating of 3.89 with a standard deviation of 0.841 for the second set of data also indicates a high level of satisfaction, with similar variability compared to the first set. The interpretation for both sets of data is "High", suggesting that the overall experience is rated positively by both students and teachers.

The data of University A showed that the mean rating for the teachers is 4.20. The standard deviation for the mean rating is 1.229, suggesting some variability in the ratings among the teachers. The mean rating of 3.50 with a standard deviation of 1.179 for the second set of data is also at a high level, although slightly lower than the first set. The interpretation for both sets of data is "High", indicating that the teachers generally rate positively.

Based on the provided data for University A students, the mean rating for the students is 4.10. The standard deviation for the mean rating is 0.852, suggesting some variability in the ratings among the students, although it is relatively low. The mean rating of 4.20 with a standard deviation of 0.696 for the second set of data is also at a high level, and the standard deviation is even lower than the first set. The interpretation for both sets of data is "High", indicating that the students generally rate positively.

The teachers of University B registered this mean rating of 3.90. The standard deviation for the mean rating is 0.738, suggesting relatively low variability in the ratings among the teachers. The mean rating of 3.90 with a standard deviation of 0.876 for the second set of data also indicates a high level of performance, albeit with slightly higher variability compared to the first set. The interpretation for both sets of data is "High", suggesting that the teachers generally rate positively.

For University B, the mean rating for the students is 3.45, indicating a relatively high level of satisfaction with their overall experience. The standard deviation for the mean rating is 0.605, suggesting low variability in the ratings among the students. The interpretation for both sets of data is "High", indicating that the students generally rate their experience positively.

The mean rating for the teachers in University B is 4.00. The standard deviation for the mean rating is 0.667, suggesting relatively low variability in the ratings among the teachers. The mean rating of 3.90 with a standard deviation of 0.876 for the second set of data also indicates a high level of performance, albeit with slightly higher variability compared to the first set. The interpretation for both sets of data is "High", suggesting that the teachers generally rate positively.

For University C, the mean rating for the students is 4.30, indicating a very high level of satisfaction with their overall experience. The standard deviation for the mean rating is 0.801, suggesting moderate variability in the ratings among the students. The mean rating of 4.20 with a standard deviation of 0.768 for the second set of data also indicates a high level of satisfaction, albeit with slightly lower variability compared to the first set. The interpretation for the first set of data is "Very High", while the interpretation for the second set is "High", suggesting that the students at University C generally rate their experience very positively.

Xu (2020) discussed the Chinese graduate students normally had problems of data analysis. From the data, we can see that the mean ratings for the different groups in the universities vary slightly, with students generally rating higher than teachers. This suggests that there are some differences in opinion or experiences among the population. This also indicates that the universities are providing a satisfactory educational experience and maintaining a positive researching environment.

2.2.6 Scientific Conclusion

Scientific conclusion ranked high as shown in Table 2-6. Both teachers and students believed "conclusion is supported by theoretical background" and "conclusion provides further understanding of the research results" were very important criteria to assess students' research paper output. Therefore, the two statements were made into the questionnaire. Table 2-6 shows the Mean and Standard Deviation of the data from teachers and students in the three target programs.

Table 2-6 Scientific Conclusion (N=90)

Items	The conclusion is supported by theoretical background		The conclusion provides further understanding of the research results	
University A teacher (N=10)	M	4.00	M	4.50
	SD	0.816	SD	0.707
	Interpretation	High	Interpretation	Very High

(to be continued)

Items	The conclusion is supported by theoretical background		The conclusion provides further understanding of the research results	
University A student (N=20)	M	4.05	M	3.95
	SD	0.887	SD	0.945
	Interpretation	High	Interpretation	High
University B teacher (N=10)	M	4.00	M	4.20
	SD	0.816	SD	1.033
	Interpretation	High	Interpretation	High
University B student (N=20)	M	3.55	M	3.55
	SD	0.605	SD	0.605
	Interpretation	High	Interpretation	High
University C teacher (N=10)	M	4.00	M	4.00
	SD	0.816	SD	0.471
	Interpretation	High	Interpretation	High
University C student (N=20)	M	4.30	M	4.40
	SD	0.733	SD	0.754
	Interpretation	Very High	Interpretation	Very High
TOTAL (N=90)	M	3.98	M	4.06
	SD	0.793	SD	0.826
	Interpretation	High	Interpretation	High

Legend: 4.21–5.00, Very High; 3.41–4.20, High; 2.61–3.40, Moderate; 1.81–2.60, Low; 1.00–1.80, Poor

The average score on the item “The conclusion is supported by theoretical background” is 3.98 with a standard deviation of 0.793. The average score on the item “The conclusion provides further understanding of the research results” is 4.06 with a standard deviation of 0.826. The data indicates that students from all universities combined performed strongly in both aspects of research evaluation, with high average scores and interpretations for both items. The standard deviations, while slightly higher than the individual university data, suggest relatively low variability in the ratings given by the 90 respondents. Overall, the data supports the conclusion that students from all universities excel in ensuring that their conclusions are supported by theoretical background and in providing further understanding of research results.

The average score for the teachers in University A on the item "The conclusion is supported by theoretical background" is 4.00 with a standard deviation of 0.816. This score corresponds to an interpretation of "High". The average score for the teachers on the item "The conclusion provides further understanding of the research results" is 4.50 with a standard deviation of 0.707. This score corresponds to an interpretation of "Very High". The data indicates that the teachers at University A believe students excel in both areas evaluated.

In University A, the average score for the students on the item "The conclusion is supported by theoretical background" is 4.05 with a standard deviation of 0.887. This score corresponds to an interpretation of "High". The average score for the students on the item "The conclusion provides further understanding of the research results" is 3.95 with a standard deviation of 0.945. This score also corresponds to an interpretation of "High". The data indicates a strong performance in these aspects of research evaluation.

The teacher data in University B has an average score on the item "The conclusion is supported by theoretical background" of 4.00 with a standard deviation of 0.816. This score corresponds to an interpretation of "High". The average score for the teachers on the item "The conclusion provides further understanding of the research results" is 4.20 with a standard deviation of 1.033. This score also corresponds to an interpretation of "High". The data indicates that the teachers at University B believe students excel in both areas evaluated.

The average score for the students in University B on the item "The conclusion is supported by theoretical background" is 3.55 with a standard deviation of 0.605. This score corresponds to an interpretation of "High". The average score for the students on the item "The conclusion provides further understanding of the research results" is 3.55 with a standard deviation of 0.605. This score also corresponds to an interpretation of "High". The data indicates a strong performance in these aspects of research evaluation.

In University C, the average score for the teachers on the item "The conclusion is supported by theoretical background" is 4.00 with a standard deviation of 0.816. This score corresponds to an interpretation of "High". The average score for the teachers on the item "The conclusion provides further understanding of the research results" is 4.00 with a standard deviation of 0.471. This score also corresponds to an interpretation of "High". The data indicates that the teachers at University C believe students excel in both areas evaluated.

Based on the data from University C, the average score for the students on the item "The conclusion is supported by theoretical background" is 4.30 with a standard deviation of 0.733. This score corresponds to an interpretation of "Very High". The average score for the students on the item "The conclusion provides further understanding of the research results" is 4.40 with a standard deviation of 0.754. This score also corresponds to an interpretation of "Very High". The data indicates a strong performance in these aspects of research evaluation.

Wang (2018) emphasized the importance of conclusion for the author to express his position and identity. emphasis on the importance of conclusions aligns with established principles in academic writing, including summarizing key points, affirming authorial voice, providing closure, addressing implications, contributing to academic discourse, and building trust and credibility. The conclusions provide an opportunity for authors to summarize the key points and findings of their work. The conclusions allow authors to assert their authorial voice and perspective. The conclusions offer closure to the reader by tying together loose ends and providing a sense of resolution. The conclusions often address the implications of the research findings and suggest avenues for future research. Therefore, well-crafted conclusions contribute to academic discourse by synthesizing existing knowledge and advancing new insights.

The data underscores the competency of students from all universities in research evaluation and highlights their ability to effectively apply theoretical knowledge and enhance the understanding of research outcomes. This strong performance bodes well for the quality of research conducted by students and reflects positively on the graduate degree research education.

2.2.7 Realistic Recommendations

Realistic recommendations ranked high as shown in Table 2-7 below. Both teachers and students believed "recommendations provide guidance for practice" and "recommendations are closely related to the shortcomings in the research" were very important criteria to assess students' research paper output. Therefore, the two statements were made into the questionnaire. Table 2-7 shows the Mean and Standard Deviation of the data from teachers and students in the three target programs.

Table 2-7 Realistic Recommendations (N=90)

Items	The recommendations provide guidance for practice		The recommendations are closely related to the shortcomings in research	
University A teacher (N-10)	M	4.10	M	4.20
	SD	0.994	SD	0.789
	Interpretation	High	Interpretation	High
University A student (N=20)	M	4.45	M	4.40
	SD	0.605	SD	0.598
	Interpretation	Very High	Interpretation	Very High
University B teacher (N=10)	M	4.10	M	4.20
	SD	0.568	SD	0.632
	Interpretation	High	Interpretation	High
University B student (N=20)	M	3.55	M	3.55
	SD	0.605	SD	0.605
	Interpretation	High	Interpretation	High
University C teacher (N=10)	M	4.10	M	3.90
	SD	0.568	SD	0.568
	Interpretation	High	Interpretation	High
University C student (N=20)	M	4.45	M	4.20
	SD	0.605	SD	0.894
	Interpretation	Very High	Interpretation	High
TOTAL (N=90)	M	4.13	M	4.07
	SD	0.722	SD	0.747
	Interpretation	High	Interpretation	High

Legend: 4.21–5.00, Very High; 3.41–4.20, High; 2.61–3.40, Moderate; 1.81–2.60, Low; 1.00–1.80, Poor.

Based on the total data for the three programs, which includes all students and teachers, for the first the overall mean rating set of data is 4.13, indicating a high level of satisfaction among both students and teachers. The standard deviation for the mean rating is 0.722, suggesting moderate variability in the ratings among the total population. The mean rating of 4.07 with a standard deviation of 0.747 for the second set of data also indicates a high level of satisfaction, with similar variability compared to the first set. The interpretation for both sets of data is "High", suggesting that the overall experience is rated positively by both students and teachers.

According to the data of University A teachers, the average rating for recommendations offering guidance in practice is 4.10, with a standard deviation of 0.994, indicating a high level of importance placed on this aspect. While the average rating for recommendation pertaining to research shortcomings is 4.20, with a standard deviation of 0.789, also reflecting a high level of emphasis on this area. University A teachers rated both items highly, indicating that they believe the recommendations provide guidance for practice and are closely related to the shortcomings in research. The mean ratings for both items are above 4, suggesting a high level of agreement or satisfaction among University A teachers regarding the quality and relevance of the recommendations.

Based on the data from University A students, the average rating for recommendations offering guidance in practice is 4.45, with a standard deviation of 0.605, indicating a very high level of importance placed on this aspect. Similarly, the average rating for recommendations pertaining to research shortcomings is 4.40, with a standard deviation of 0.598, also reflecting a very high level of emphasis on this area. University A students highly rated both items, indicating their belief that the recommendations offer practical guidance and are relevant to research shortcomings. The mean ratings for both items exceed 4.4, implying strong agreement and satisfaction among University A students with the recommendations' quality and applicability.

The average rating of the teachers from University B for recommendations offering guidance in practice is 4.10, with a standard deviation of 0.568, indicating a high level of importance placed on this aspect. Similarly, the average rating for recommendations pertaining to research shortcomings is 4.20, with a standard deviation of 0.632, also reflecting a high level of emphasis on this area. University B teachers rated both items highly, indicating their perception that the recommendations offer valuable practical guidance and are relevant to research shortcomings. The mean ratings for both items are above 4.0, suggesting a high level of agreement and satisfaction among University B teachers regarding the quality and relevance of the recommendations.

From the students of University B, the average rating for recommendations offering guidance in practice is 3.55, with a standard deviation of 0.605, indicating a high level of importance placed on this aspect. Similarly, the average rating for recommendations pertaining to research shortcomings is 3.55, with a standard deviation of 0.605, also reflecting a high level of emphasis on this area. University B students rate both items as high, indicating their perception that the recommendations offer valuable practical guidance and are relevant to research shortcomings. The mean ratings for both items are at 3.55, suggesting a moderate level of agreement and satisfaction among University B students regarding the quality and relevance of the recommendations.

As rated by teachers from University C, the average rating for recommendations offering guidance in practice is 4.10, with a standard deviation of 0.568, indicating a high level of importance placed on this aspect, while the average rating for recommendations pertaining to research shortcomings is 3.90, with a standard deviation of 0.568, also reflecting a high level of emphasis on this area. The data suggests that University C teachers highly value the recommendations for their practical guidance in practice and their relevance to addressing research shortcomings. The consistent and positive responses from the teachers indicate a strong endorsement of the quality and utility of the recommendations within this group.

The data of University C students show that the average rating for recommendations offering guidance in practice is 4.45, with a standard deviation of 0.605, indicating a very high level of importance placed on this aspect. The average rating for recommendations pertaining to research shortcomings is 4.20, with a standard deviation of 0.894, also reflecting a high level of emphasis on this area. The low standard deviations indicate that there was relatively little variability in responses for both items, suggesting a strong level of agreement among the student responses from University C.

Cargill, Gao, Wang and O'Connor (2018) discussed when advanced graduate students actually wrote papers, recommendations could be drawn based on the literature, providing empirical evidence, theoretical support, qualitative insights, comparative analysis, expert opinions, and historical context. If the discussion is grounded in theoretical frameworks or models, citations to related literature can offer theoretical support for the recommendations. Qualitative research exploring the experiences and practices of advanced graduate students in writing papers can provide rich insights that complement the recommendations. Citations to works authored by experts in the field can bolster the credibility of the recommendations.

As can be seen from the above data, target graduate students highly value practical guidance in their academic or research endeavors. This suggests that students appreciate recommendations that can help them apply theoretical knowledge in real-world settings or practical contexts. Target graduate students place on the limitations or gaps in research. This emphasis on acknowledging and addressing research weaknesses could indicate a strong commitment to critical thinking and improvement in research practices among the students.

2.2.8 Writing Format

Writing format ranked high as shown in Table 2-8 below. Both teachers and students believed "capitalization, spelling and punctuation have no problem" and "paper format and reference are standardized" were very important criteria to assess students' research paper output. Therefore, they were made into the questionnaire. Table 2-8 shows the Mean and Standard Deviation of the data from teachers and students in the three target programs.

Table 2-8 Writing Format (N=90)

Items	The capitalization, spelling and punctuation have no problem		The paper format and reference are standardized	
University A teacher (N=10)	M	4.20	M	4.40
	SD	1.229	SD	0.966
	Interpretation	High	Interpretation	Very High
University A student (N=20)	M	5.00	M	4.80
	SD	0.000	SD	0.410
	Interpretation	Very High	Interpretation	Very High

(*to be continued*)

Items	The capitalization, spelling and punctuation have no problem		The paper format and reference are standardized	
University B teacher (N=10)	M	4.20	M	4.20
	SD	0.789	SD	0.919
	Interpretation	High	Interpretation	High
University B student (N=20)	M	3.75	M	3.80
	SD	0.716	SD	0.616
	Interpretation	High	Interpretation	High
University C teacher (N=10)	M	4.30	M	4.30
	SD	0.675	SD	0.675
	Interpretation	Very High	Interpretation	Very High
University C student (N=20)	M	4.35	M	4.50
	SD	0.813	SD	0.607
	Interpretation	Very High	Interpretation	Very High
TOTAL (N=90)	M	4.32	M	4.34
	SD	0.832	SD	0.737
	Interpretation	Very High	Interpretation	Very High

Legend: 4.21–5.00, Very High; 3.41–4.20, High; 2.61–3.40, Moderate; 1.81–2.60, Low; 1.00–1.80, Poor.

Based on the total data for the three programs, which includes all students and teachers, the overall mean rating for the first set of data is 4.32, indicating a very high level of satisfaction among both students and teachers. The standard deviation for the mean rating is 0.832, suggesting moderate variability in the ratings among the total population. The mean rating of 4.34 with a standard deviation of 0.737 for the second set of data also indicates a very high level of satisfaction, with similar variability compared to the first set. It seems like the students across all universities generally have higher means compared to the teachers based on the provided data.

From University A teachers' responses, the average rating for capitalization, spelling and punctuation is 4.20, with a standard deviation of 1.229. The average rating for paper format and reference is 4.40, with a standard deviation of 0.966. The interpretation suggests that the teachers believed that students from University A performed at a high level in terms of capitalization, spelling, and punctuation, while their performance in the paper format and reference standardization is even higher, with a very high rating.

University A students registered an average rating for capitalization, spelling and punctuation of 5.00, with a standard deviation of 0.000. The average rating for paper format and reference is 4.80, with a standard deviation of 0.410. The interpretation suggests that the students from University A performed exceptionally well in both capitalization, spelling, and punctuation as well as paper format and reference standardization, with both categories receiving a "Very High" rating.

Based on the teachers' data from University B, the average rating for capitalization, spelling and punctuation is 4.20, with a standard deviation of 0.789. The average rating for paper format and reference is 4.20, with a standard deviation of 0.919. The interpretation indicates that the teachers from University B scored students at a "High" level in both capitalization, spelling, and punctuation as well as paper format and reference standardization.

The students of University B got an average rating of 3.75 for capitalization, spelling and punctuation, with a standard deviation of 0.716. The average rating for paper format and reference is 3.80, with a standard deviation of 0.616. The interpretation implies that the students from University B scored at a "High" level in both capitalization, spelling, and punctuation as well as paper format and reference standardization.

According to the responses of teachers from University C, the average rating for capitalization, spelling and punctuation is 4.30, with a standard deviation of 0.675. The average rating for paper format and reference is also 4.30, with a standard deviation of 0.675. The interpretation indicates that the teachers from University C scored at a "Very High" level the students in both capitalization, spelling, and punctuation as well as paper format and reference standardization.

As rated by University C students, the average rating for capitalization, spelling and punctuation is 4.35, with a standard deviation of 0.813. The average rating for paper format and reference is 4.50, with a standard deviation of 0.607. The interpretation indicates that the students from University C scored at a "Very High" level in both capitalization, spelling, and punctuation as well as paper format and reference standardization.

In a nutshell, the data provided highlights the strong performance of students in terms of writing format on capitalization, spelling, punctuation, paper format, and reference standardization as perceived by both students and teachers. This accords with the idea of Liu (2005) that standardized writing formats contribute to a positive academic environment that supports research paper writing. Citations to professional standards and guidelines in academic writing can underscore the importance of standardized formats in maintaining quality and consistency in scholarly communication. References to style manuals, editorial guidelines, and academic publishing standards can highlight the institutional support for standardized formats in promoting a positive academic environment (American Psychological Association, 2020).

2.2.9 Summary

Table 2-9 shows the summary of research performance of graduate students in research paper output. The overall mean score across all indicators is 4.07 with a standard deviation of 0.807, indicating a high level of performance in the research project as a whole.

Table 2-9 Summary Table of Student Research Performance of Research Paper Output

Indicators	Mean	SD	Interpretation
Thesis topic selection	4.12	0.762	High
	4.14	0.787	High
Academic values	3.93	0.832	High
	3.93	0.946	High
Updated theories	4.09	0.774	High
	4.04	0.763	High
Appropriate research methods	3.97	0.917	High
	4.11	0.785	High
Analysis skills	3.98	0.848	High
	3.89	0.841	High
Scientific conclusion	3.98	0.793	High
	4.06	0.826	High
Realistic recommendations	4.13	0.722	High
	4.07	0.747	High
Writing format	4.32	0.832	Very High
	4.34	0.737	Very High
Overall mean	4.07	0.807	High

Legend: 4.21–5.00, Very High; 3.41–4.20, High; 2.61–3.40, Moderate; 1.80–2.60, Low; 1.00–1.80, Poor

Summarily, the data suggests that the research programs have excelled in various key areas such as thesis topic selection, academic values, updated theories, research methods, analysis skills, scientific conclusion, realistic recommendations, and writing format. These high scores indicate a strong and well-executed research project that adheres to academic standards and best practices.

2.3 Research Defense Based on Viva Standards

According to the pre-survey, the research defense based on viva standards was mostly related to answering viewpoint, language expression ability, mastering basic knowledge, and independent research ability perspectives. Reporting data of the teacher questionnaires presented divergences.

2.3.1 Answering Viewpoint

Answering viewpoint ranked firstly high in the pre-survey result. Both teachers and students believed "answering viewpoint is correct" and "answering viewpoint is logical" were very important criteria to assess students' research paper output. Therefore, they were made into the questionnaire. Table 2-10 shows the Mean and Standard Deviation of the data from teachers and students in the three target programs.

Table 2-10 Answering Viewpoint (N=90)

Items	The answering viewpoint is correct		The answering viewpoint is logical	
University A teacher (N=10)	M	4.40	M	4.30
	SD	0.843	SD	0.949
	Interpretation	Very High	Interpretation	Very High
University A student (N=20)	M	4.60	M	4.55
	SD	0.503	SD	0.510
	Interpretation	Very High	Interpretation	Very High

(*to be continued*)

Items	The answering viewpoint is correct		The answering viewpoint is logical	
University B teacher (N=10)	M	4.10	M	4.10
	SD	0.738	SD	0.876
	Interpretation	High	Interpretation	High
University B student (N=20)	M	3.55	M	3.50
	SD	0.605	SD	0.607
	Interpretation	High	Interpretation	High
University C teacher (N=10)	M	4.10	M	4.20
	SD	0.568	SD	0.632
	Interpretation	High	Interpretation	High
University C student (N=20)	M	4.15	M	4.20
	SD	0.875	SD	0.834
	Interpretation	High	Interpretation	High
TOTAL (N=90)	M	4.13	M	4.12
	SD	0.767	SD	0.791
	Interpretation	High	Interpretation	High

Legend: 4.21–5.00, Very High; 3.41–4.20, High; 2.61–3.40, Moderate; 1.81–2.60, Low; 1.00–1.80, Poor.

Based on the total data for the three programs, which includes all students and teachers, mean overall rating for "answering viewpoint is correct" is 4.13, indicating a high level of satisfaction among both students and teachers. The standard deviation for the mean rating is 0.767, suggesting moderate variability in the ratings among the total population. The mean rating of 4.12 with a standard deviation of 0.791 for "answering viewpoint is logical" also indicates a high level of satisfaction, with similar variability compared to the first statement.

From the data from teachers of University A, the average rating for answering viewpoint is correct is 4.40, with a standard deviation of 0.843. The average rating for answering viewpoint is logical is 4.30, with a standard deviation of 0.949. Based on the data from University A, teachers consistently rate the correctness and logic of the answering viewpoint very high, with minimal variability in their ratings for correctness and some variability for logic. This indicates a strong consensus among the teachers at University A regarding the quality of the answering viewpoint by students in terms of correctness and logic.

The average rating for "University A students answering viewpoint is correct" is 4.60, with a standard deviation of 0.503. The average rating for "answering viewpoint is logical" is 4.55, with a standard deviation of 0.510. Based on the data from University A, students consistently rate the correctness and logic of the answering viewpoint quite high in their responses, with minimal variability in their ratings for both aspects. This indicates a strong consensus among the students at University A regarding the quality of the answering viewpoint in terms of correctness and logic in their responses.

The data from University B reveals that there are a total of 10 valid teachers responses for the two statements. The average rating for answering viewpoint is correct is 4.10, with a standard deviation of 0.738. The average rating for answering viewpoint is logical is 4.10, with a standard deviation of 0.876. Based on the data from University B, teachers provide generally positive ratings for both the correctness and logic of the answering viewpoint in their responses. However, there is more variability in how teachers at University B rate the logic of the answering viewpoint compared to the correctness, indicating a wider range of opinions among the teachers regarding the logic of the answering viewpoint.

The data from University B provides that there are a total of 20 valid students responses for the two statements. The average rating for answering viewpoint is correct is 3.55, with a standard deviation of 0.605. The average rating for answering viewpoint is logical is 3.50, with a standard deviation of 0.607. Based on the data from University B, students provide moderately positive ratings for both the correctness and logic of the answering viewpoint in their responses. There is variability in how students at University B rate both the correctness and logic of the answering viewpoint, indicating a range of opinions among the students regarding the correctness and logic of the answering viewpoint.

The data of University C shows that there are a total of 10 valid teachers responses for the two statements. The average rating for answering viewpoint is correct is 4.10, with a standard deviation of 0.568. The average rating for answering viewpoint is logical is 4.20, with a standard deviation of 0.632. Based on the data from University C, teachers provide positive ratings for both the correctness and logic of the answering viewpoint in their responses. There is some variability in how teachers at University C rate both the correctness and logic of the answering viewpoint, suggesting differing opinions among the teachers regarding the correctness and logic of the answering viewpoint.

The data from University C indicates there are a total of 20 valid students responses for the two statements. The average rating for answering viewpoint is correct is 4.15, with a standard deviation of 0.875. The average rating for answering viewpoint is logical is 4.20, with a standard deviation of 0.834. Based on the data from University C, students provide generally positive ratings for both the correctness and logic of the answering viewpoint in their responses. There is some variability in how students at University C rate both the correctness and logic of the answering viewpoint, suggesting differing opinions among the students regarding the correctness and logic of the answering viewpoint.

The data regarding the ratings given by teachers and students for the correctness and logic of the answering viewpoint in student responses provides valuable insights. Overall, the data highlights the importance of consistency in evaluating student responses and the subjectivity inherent in assessing correctness and logic. It also underscores the need for clear and consistent criteria for evaluating student work to ensure fairness and accuracy in grading.

Xu (2020) emphasized on the correctness and logic of graduate students' thesis defense. Xu's emphasis on correctness and logic in graduate students' thesis defense can strengthen the argument, provide a scholarly basis for the claim. Best practices in graduate education can offer insights into effective strategies for teaching and assessing correctness and logic in academic writing and presentation.

2.3.2 Language Expression Ability

Language expression ability ranked secondly high in the pre-survey result. Both teachers and students believed "language expression is fluent" and "pronunciation is clear" were very important criteria to assess students' research paper output. Therefore, they were made into the questionnaire. Table 2-11 shows the Mean and Standard Deviation of the data from teachers and students in the three target programs.

Table 2-11 Language Expression Ability (N=90)

Items	The language expression is fluent		The pronunciation is clear	
University A teacher (N=10)	M	4.00	M	4.00
	SD	0.667	SD	0.667
	Interpretation	High	Interpretation	High

(*to be continued*)

Items	The language expression is fluent		The pronunciation is clear	
University A student (N=20)	M	4.50	M	4.40
	SD	0.513	SD	0.598
	Interpretation	Very High	Interpretation	Very High
University B teacher (N=10)	M	4.10	M	4.30
	SD	0.876	SD	0.823
	Interpretation	High	Interpretation	Very High
University B student (N=20)	M	3.60	M	3.60
	SD	0.681	SD	0.598
	Interpretation	High	Interpretation	High
University C teacher (N=10)	M	4.30	M	4.30
	SD	0.675	SD	0.675
	Interpretation	Very High	Interpretation	Very High
University C student (N=20)	M	4.25	M	4.30
	SD	0.716	SD	0.801
	Interpretation	Very High	Interpretation	Very High
TOTAL (N=90)	M	4.12	M	4.13
	SD	0.732	SD	0.737
	Interpretation	High	Interpretation	High

Legend: 4.21–5.00, Very High; 3.41–4.20, High; 2.61–3.40, Moderate; 1.81–2.60, Low; 1.00–1.80, Poor.

Based on the total data for the three programs, which includes all students and teachers, mean overall rating for "language expression is fluent" is 4.12. The standard deviation for the mean rating is 0.732, suggesting moderate variability in the ratings among the total population. The mean rating of 4.13 with a standard deviation of 0.737 for "pronunciation is clear". The interpretation of the data for the total population indicates that the participants in the three programs are generally perceived to have high levels of fluent language expression and clear pronunciation, with some variability in these perceptions among the raters.

Based on the data provided for University A teacher ratings with a mean rating of 4.00 for both statements, along with standard deviations of 0.667 for both measures, the teacher ratings for language expression and pronunciation are high. The mean ratings suggest that the teachers perceive their students to have fluent language expression and clear pronunciation. The standard deviations indicate that there is moderate variability in the ratings provided by the teachers, suggesting some differences in perceptions among them.

Based on the data provided for University A student ratings with a mean rating of 4.50 for "language expression is fluent" and 4.40 for "pronunciation is clear", along with standard deviations of 0.513 and 0.598 for the respective measures. The interpretation is that the student ratings for language expression and pronunciation at University A are very high. The high mean ratings and standard deviations suggest a strong consensus among the students regarding the language skills of their peers.

Based on the data provided for University B teacher ratings with a mean rating of 4.10 for "language expression is fluent" and 4.30 for "pronunciation is clear", along with standard deviations of 0.876 and 0.823 for the respective measures. The interpretation is that the teacher ratings for language expression and pronunciation at University B are high and very high, respectively. The mean ratings suggest that, on average, the teachers at University B perceive their students to have high language expression skills and very clear pronunciation. The higher mean rating for pronunciation compared to language expression indicates that teachers may find pronunciation skills to be stronger among their students. The standard deviations suggest some variability in the ratings provided by the teachers, indicating differing perceptions among them, especially for language expression.

Based on the data provided for University B student ratings with a mean rating of 3.60 for "language expression is fluent" and 3.60 for "pronunciation is clear", along with standard deviations of 0.681 and 0.598 for the respective measures, the interpretation is that the student ratings for language expression and pronunciation at University B are high for both aspects. The mean ratings indicate that, on average, the students at University B perceive their peers to have high language expression skills and clear pronunciation skills. The equal mean ratings for both aspects suggest that students view both language expression and pronunciation similarly in terms of proficiency. The standard deviations indicate some variability in the ratings provided by the students, suggesting that there may be differing opinions or perceptions among them regarding their peers' language skills.

Based on the data provided for University C teacher ratings with a mean rating of 4.30 for "language expression skills" and 4.30 for "pronunciation skills", along with standard deviations of 0.675 for both measures, the interpretation is that the teacher ratings of students at University C are very high for both language expression and pronunciation skills. The mean ratings indicate that, on average, the teachers at University C perceive their students to have very high proficiency in both aspects. The equal mean ratings for language expression and pronunciation suggest that teachers view both skills as equally strong among their students. The standard deviations suggest some consistency in the ratings provided by the teachers, with relatively low variability in their perceptions of students' language skills.

Based on the data provided for University C student ratings with a mean rating of 4.25 for "language expression skills" and 4.30 for "pronunciation skills", along with standard deviations of 0.716 for language expression and 0.801 for pronunciation, the interpretation is that the student ratings at University C are very high for both language expression and pronunciation skills. The mean ratings indicate that, on average, the students at University C have very high proficiency in both aspects. The standard deviations indicate some variability in the ratings provided by the students, suggesting that there may be differing opinions or perceptions among them regarding their peers' language skills.

Diverse disciplines such as linguistics, rhetoric, or cognitive science can offer a multidimensional view of the importance of correctness and logic in thesis defense. Citations to professional standards and guidelines in academia can underscore the significance of correctness and logic in thesis defense. References to ethical codes, disciplinary norms, or institutional guidelines can reinforce the argument by highlighting the expectations and standards upheld by the academic community (American Psychological Association, 2020).

2.3.3 Mastering Basic Knowledge

Mastering basic knowledge ranked thirdly high in the pre-survey result. Both teachers and students believed "master basic knowledge of the English subject" and "master basic knowledge of the research topic" were very important criteria to assess students' research paper output. Therefore, they were made into the questionnaire. Table 2-12 shows the Mean and Standard Deviation of the data from teachers and students in the three target programs.

Table 2-12 Mastering Basic Knowledge (N=90)

Items	Master basic knowledge of the English subject		Master basic knowledge of the research topic	
University A teacher (N=10)	M	4.60	M	4.60
	SD	0.843	SD	0. 843
	Interpretation	Very High	Interpretation	Very High
University A student (N=20)	M	4.55	M	4.60
	SD	0.510	SD	0.503
	Interpretation	Very High	Interpretation	Very High
University B teacher (N=10)	M	4.40	M	4.40
	SD	0.699	SD	0.516
	Interpretation	High	Interpretation	High
University B student (N=20)	M	3.90	M	3.90
	SD	0.641	SD	0.641
	Interpretation	High	Interpretation	High
University C teacher (N=10)	M	4.40	M	4.30
	SD	0.699	SD	0.675
	Interpretation	Very High	Interpretation	Very High
University C student (N=20)	M	4.40	M	4.40
	SD	0.754	SD	0.754
	Interpretation	Very High	Interpretation	Very High
TOTAL (N=90)	M	4.34	M	4.34
	SD	0.706	SD	0.690
	Interpretation	Very High	Interpretation	Very High

Legend: 4.21–5.00, Very High; 3.41–4.20, High; 2.61–3.40, Moderate; 1.81–2.60, Low; 1.00–1.80, Poor.

For the total sample of 90 participants (combining teachers and students from all three universities), the mean ratings for mastery of basic knowledge of the English subject and the research topic are both 4.34, indicating a very high level of mastery according to the interpretation scale. The standard deviations of 0.706 and 0.690 for these aspects suggest that there is some variability in the ratings provided by the participants, although it still falls within the very high level of agreement among them in their assessment of mastery.

For University A teachers, the mean ratings for mastery of basic knowledge of the English subject and the research topic are both 4.60, indicating a very high level of mastery according to the interpretation scale. The standard deviation of 0.843 suggests that there is relatively low variability in the ratings provided by the teachers, indicating a high level of agreement among them in their assessment of mastery.

The data of University A students shows, the mean ratings for mastery of basic knowledge of the English subject and the research topic are 4.55 and 4.60, respectively, indicating a very high level of mastery according to the interpretation scale. The standard deviations of 0.510 and 0.503 for these aspects suggest that there is relatively low variability in the ratings provided by the students, indicating a high level of agreement among them in their assessment of mastery.

The data from University B teachers illustrates that the mean ratings for mastery of basic knowledge of the English subject and the research topic are both 4.40, indicating a high level of mastery according to the interpretation scale. The standard deviations of 0.699 and 0.516 for these aspects suggest that there is some variability in the ratings provided by the teachers, although it still falls within the high level of agreement among them in their assessment of mastery.

According to the data from University B students, the mean ratings for mastery of basic knowledge of the English subject and the research topic are both 3.90, indicating a high level of mastery according to the interpretation scale. The standard deviations of 0.641 for both aspects suggest that there is some variability in the ratings provided by the students, yet it still falls within the high level of agreement among them in their assessment of mastery.

According to the data provided by University C teachers, the mean ratings for mastery of basic knowledge of the English subject and the research topic are 4.40 and 4.30, respectively, indicating a very high level of mastery according to the interpretation scale. The standard deviations of 0.699 and 0.675 for these aspects suggest that there is relatively low variability in the ratings provided by the teachers, indicating a high level of agreement among them in their assessment of mastery.

From University C students data, the mean ratings for mastery of basic knowledge of the English subject and the research topic are both 4.40, indicating a very high level of mastery according to the interpretation scale. The standard deviations of 0.754 for both aspects suggest that there is some variability in the ratings provided by the students, yet it still falls within the very high level of agreement among them in their assessment of mastery.

The data presented show consistently high levels of mastery in both basic knowledge of the English subject and the research topic across different groups within the universities. Overall, the data indicate that both teachers and students across the universities have a strong command of the basic knowledge of the English subject and the research topic. This consistency in high ratings across different groups suggests a shared understanding and agreement on the level of mastery demonstrated by the participants.

Basic knowledge is one of the important elements assessing the research performance of China's English major graduate students (Zhang & Deng, 2019). The significance of basic knowledge in assessing research performance in English major graduate students can be underscored within the broader academic discourse. By demonstrating the claim about the importance of basic knowledge in assessing research performance, the argument becomes more robust and trustworthy.

2.3.4 Independent Research Ability

Independent research ability ranked high in the pre-survey result. Both teachers and students believed "evaluate different views and form independent judgments" and "identify problems and propose innovative solutions" were very important criteria to assess students' research paper output. Therefore, they were made into the questionnaire. Table 2-13 shows the Mean and Standard Deviation of the data from teachers and students in the three target programs.

Table 2-13 Independent Research Ability (N=90)

Items	Evaluate different views and form independent judgments		Identify problems and propose innovative solutions	
University A teacher (N=10)	M	4.30	M	4.30
	SD	0.949	SD	0.949
	Interpretation	Very High	Interpretation	Very High

(*to be continued*)

Items	Evaluate different views and form independent judgments		Identify problems and propose innovative solutions	
University A student (N=20)	M	4.35	M	4.05
	SD	0.489	SD	0.759
	Interpretation	Very High	Interpretation	High
University B teacher (N=10)	M	3.90	M	3.90
	SD	0.994	SD	1.101
	Interpretation	High	Interpretation	High
University B student (N=20)	M	3.65	M	3.60
	SD	0.587	SD	0.598
	Interpretation	High	Interpretation	High
University C teacher (N=10)	M	4.40	M	4.20
	SD	0.966	SD	0.632
	Interpretation	Very High	Interpretation	High
University C student (N=20)	M	4.25	M	4.25
	SD	0.786	SD	0.716
	Interpretation	Very High	Interpretation	Very High
TOTAL (N=90)	M	4.12	M	4.02
	SD	0.791	SD	0.793
	Interpretation	High	Interpretation	High

Legend: 4.21–5.00, Very High; 3.41–4.20, High; 2.61–3.40, Moderate; 1.81–2.60, Low; 1.00–1.80, Poor.

For the total sample of 90 participants (combining University A, B, and C), the mean ratings for evaluating different views and forming independent judgments is 4.12, and for identifying problems and proposing innovative solutions is 4.02. The standard deviations for these ratings are 0.791 and 0.793, respectively. This suggests a high level of performance in both skills across the entire sample.

The data from University A teachers illustrates that the mean ratings for evaluating different views and forming independent judgments and identifying problems and proposing innovative solutions are both 4.30, with a standard deviation of 0.949. These results suggest a very high level of competency in both skills at University A.

According to the collected data from University A students, the mean ratings for evaluating different views and forming independent judgments (4.35) and identifying problems and proposing innovative solutions (4.05) indicate a very high and high level of performance, respectively. The standard deviations for these ratings are 0.489 and 0.759, reflecting consistency in ratings across the student cohort.

Based on the data collected of University B teachers, the data shows a mean rating of 3.90 for both evaluating different views and forming independent judgments, as well as for identifying problems and proposing innovative solutions. The standard deviations for these ratings are 0.994 and 1.101, respectively. This indicates a high level of performance in these skills at University B.

In light of the data provided by University B students, the mean ratings for evaluating different views and forming independent judgments is 3.65, and for identifying problems and proposing innovative solutions is 3.60. The standard deviations for these ratings are 0.587 and 0.598, respectively. This suggests a high level of performance in these skills among the students at University B.

Based on the data from University C teachers, the mean rating for evaluating different views and forming independent judgments is 4.40, and for identifying problems and proposing innovative solutions is 4.20. The standard deviations for these ratings are 0.966 and 0.632, respectively. This indicates a very high level of competency in evaluating different views and forming independent judgments, and a high level of competency in identifying problems and proposing innovative solutions among the teachers at University C.

Based on the data from University C students, the mean ratings for evaluating different views and forming independent judgments is 4.25, and for identifying problems and proposing innovative solutions is 4.25. The standard deviations for these ratings are 0.786 and 0.716, respectively. This indicates a very high level of performance in both skills among the students at University C.

Based on the data provided for University A, B, and C, it is evident that there is a consistently high level of competency in the skills of evaluating different views and forming independent judgments, as well as identifying problems and proposing innovative solutions among both students and teachers across these institutions.

Specifically, University C stands out with very high ratings for both teachers and students in these skills, showcasing a strong emphasis on critical thinking and problem-solving abilities within their academic community. Critical thinking skills and innovative problem-solving approaches are essential for success in both academic and professional settings (Kabyltaevna et al., 2022). Emphasis on critical thinking and problem-solving abilities with citations to related literature can validate the findings, contextualize them within the academic discourse, enhance credibility, and encourage the adoption of best practices in academia.

University B also demonstrates high performance levels in these areas, indicating a solid foundation in these essential competencies among their students and teachers. University A, although not explicitly mentioned in the summary, likely falls within a similar range of competency based on the overall interpretation of the total sample data.

The relatively low standard deviations across the board suggest a level of consistency in the ratings, indicating a general consensus among the participants regarding their proficiency in these skills. This consistency further reinforces the notion that critical thinking and problem-solving abilities are valued and actively cultivated within the academic environments of these universities.

2.3.5 Summary

Table 2-14 shows the summary of research performance of graduate students in research oral defense (viva). The overall mean score across all indicators is 4.17 with a standard deviation of 0.751, indicating a high level of performance in the research project as a whole.

Table 2-14 Summary Table of Student Research Performance of Research Oral Defense

Indicators	Mean	SD	Interpretation
Answering Viewpoint	4.13 4.12	0.767 0.791	High High
Language Expression Ability	4.12 4.13	0.732 0.737	High High
Mastering Basic Knowledge	4.34 4.34	0.706 0.690	Very High Very High
Independent Research Ability	4.12 4.02	0.791 0.793	High High
Overall Mean	4.17	0.751	High

Legend: 4.21–5.00, Very High; 3.41–4.20, High; 2.61–3.40, Moderate; 1.80–2.60, Low; 1.00–1.80, Poor

As can be seen, the data underscores the target programs' commitment to cultivating critical thinking and problem-solving abilities among its students. The high to very high ratings across key indicators reflect the institution's success in equipping students with essential skills for academic and professional success. By excelling in these areas, students are better prepared to tackle complex challenges, think critically, and make informed decisions in various contexts.

2.4 The Interview Data Report

2.4.1 Evaluation of the English Grad School Research Output

The interview data took form through the thematic organization of the interview content. After the thematic analysis of the data of the interview participants by NVivo, the Final Themes generated by the interview content of the participants were "Research Output". Among them, the final theme can be divided into 4 Initial Themes, as shown in Table 2-15.

Table 2-15 Themes on "The Research Output"

Questions	Codes	Initial Themes	Final Themes
How do you evaluate the English grad school research output?	originality and contribution, quality of writing and presentation, responds to feedback, ethical guidelines, academic integrity, and professional standards, clarity and coherence, depth of analysis, originality and contribution, methodological rigor, quality of writing and presentation	Collaborations	Research Output
		Research Impact	
		Innovation and Originality	
		Feedback and Reviews	

Teachers have positive evaluation of the research output. However, they have divergent preferences of their evaluation of the research output. By evaluating these aspects of a student's research output in an English graduate program, teachers hope to provide constructive feedback, identify strengths and areas for improvement, and help the graduate students develop the skills and competencies necessary for producing high-quality research in the field of English studies.

For example, some teachers would like to evaluate the scope, depth, and coherence of the student's research project. They consider whether the research question is clearly defined, the methodology is appropriate, and the conclusions are well-supported by evidence. Some teachers would like to assess how well the student engages with existing scholarship in their field through a comprehensive literature review. They look for evidence of critical analysis, synthesis of key ideas, and identification of gaps or opportunities for further research. Some teachers would like to evaluate the rigor and appropriateness of the research methodology employed by the student. They consider whether the research design is well-structured, data collection methods are sound, and analysis techniques are appropriate for the research question.

Some teachers would like to consider the originality and contribution of the student's research to the field of English studies. They assess whether the research offers new insights, challenges existing assumptions, or opens up new avenues for future research. Some teachers would like to evaluate the quality of the student's writing and presentation of their research. They consider factors such as clarity, coherence, organization, and adherence to academic conventions. They hope to assess whether the research is effectively communicated to the reader or audience. Some teachers would like to consider how the student responds to feedback from advisors, committee members, and peers. They evaluate their ability to incorporate feedback into their research, revise their work effectively, and demonstrate a willingness to learn and improve. Some teachers would like to assess the student's adherence to ethical guidelines, academic integrity, and professional standards in conducting and reporting their research. They consider factors such as proper citation practices, respect for intellectual property rights, and responsible conduct of research.

When teachers have divergent reports of their evaluation of a student's research output, it can be a challenging situation to navigate. Here are some potential reasons why teachers may have differing opinions on the evaluation.

Firstly, evaluation of research output can be subjective, as different teachers have varying preferences, perspectives, and criteria for assessing research quality. This subjectivity can lead to divergent reports based on individual interpretations and priorities. Teachers have different expectations regarding the depth, breadth, and originality of the research output. Variances in expectations can result in varying assessments of the research contribution and overall quality.

Secondly, teachers have different expectations regarding the depth, breadth, and originality of the research output. Variances in expectations can result in varying assessments of the research contribution and overall quality.

Thirdly, teachers have different methodological preferences or biases that influence their assessment of the research. Variances in methodological rigor, data analysis techniques, or research design can lead to divergent evaluations.

Fourthly, teachers interpret the research findings differently based on their own expertise, background knowledge, and theoretical perspectives. This can result in differing assessments of the significance and implications of the research.

Fifthly, differences in how teachers provide feedback to students and communicate their evaluation criteria can also contribute to divergent reports. Clear communication and alignment on evaluation criteria are essential to ensure consistency in assessment.

Sixthly, personal relationships, dynamics, or biases between teachers and students may also influence the evaluation process. It is important for teachers to remain objective and focus on the research quality rather than personal factors.

To address divergent reports in the evaluation of research output, it may be beneficial to promote open communication among teachers, clarify evaluation criteria and expectations, encourage constructive feedback, and seek consensus on assessment standards. Collaboration and dialogue among teachers can help ensure a fair and consistent evaluation process for students' research outputs.

Students have good evaluation of their research output. They also have divergent preferences of their evaluation of the research output, which shares some similarity with the teachers. They would approach the evaluation of research output with a critical and discerning eye, seeking to assess the strengths and weaknesses of the research in relation to established scholarly standards and expectations in the field of English studies.

For example, some students think it is important to assess the clarity and coherence of the research output, including the organization of ideas, logical flow of arguments, and coherence of the overall research. They believe a well-structured and clearly presented research output is essential for effective communication of ideas.

Some student thinks it is important to evaluate the depth of analysis in the research output, including the extent to which the research engages with relevant theoretical frameworks, critically evaluates existing scholarship, and provides insightful interpretations of the research data or texts under study.

Some students think it is important to consider the originality and contribution of the research output to the field of English studies. They would look for evidence of new insights, innovative approaches, or novel interpretations that advance scholarly understanding in the discipline.

Some student thinks it is important to assess the methodological rigor of the research output, including the appropriateness of the research design and methodology for addressing the research question, the thoroughness of data collection and analysis processes, and the soundness of the overall research methodology.

Some students think it is important to evaluate the quality of writing and presentation in the research output, including the clarity of language, effectiveness of argumentation, and adherence to academic conventions of style and citation. They believe a well-written and professionally presented research output is crucial for academic credibility.

Some students think it is important to consider the student's engagement with feedback from professors, peers, and other reviewers. They believe demonstrating a willingness to receive and incorporate feedback, engage in scholarly dialogue, and revise the research output based on constructive criticism is a sign of intellectual growth and development.

It is true that students have different preferences when it comes to the evaluation of their research output. As an evaluator, it is important to be mindful of these divergent preferences and to tailor feedback accordingly. This involve discussing expectations and preferences with the student at the outset of the evaluation process, seeking feedback from the student on their preferred style of feedback, and being open to adjusting approach based on the student's feedback.

Nir and Bogler (2021) discussed Candidates' engagement in academic argument, as well as design/methodology/approach were significant in assessing their research performance. This is consistent to the interview data.

Ultimately, the goal of evaluation is to support the student's growth and development as a researcher and scholar. By being responsive to students' preferences and needs, evaluators can create a more supportive and effective learning environment that fosters student success and academic excellence.

2.4.2 Evaluation of the English Grad School Performance Based on Viva Standards

Through the thematic organizing the interview content, the interview data were formed. After the thematic analysis of the data of the interview participants by NVivo, the Final Themes generated by the interview content of the participants were "Research Performance Based on Viva Standards". Among them, the final theme can be divided into 5 Initial Themes, as shown in Table 2-16.

Table 2-16 Themes on "Research Performance Based on Viva Standards"

Questions	Codes	Initial Themes	Final Themes
How do you evaluate the English grad school performance based on viva standards?	originality and significance, depth of understanding of the relevant literature, critically analyze and interpret their research findings, examine the appropriateness and effectiveness of the research methodology, ability to communicate research effectively during the viva, adherence to ethical guidelines, academic integrity, and professional standards throughout the viva process, overall demeanor, professionalism, and confidence, communication skills, depth of knowledge, research skills	Engagement with Literature	Research Performance Based on Viva Standards
		Methodological Rigor	
		Presentation and Defense	
		Contribution to Field	
		Feedback and Improvement	

Teachers have positive evaluation of the research performance based on viva standards. They also have divergent preferences of their evaluation of the research performance based on viva standards. By considering these viva standards, teachers hope to provide comprehensive feedback to students, identify areas of strength and areas for improvement, and make informed decisions regarding their readiness for completion of the English graduate program.

For example, some teachers would like to assess the originality and significance of the student's research contribution. They look for evidence that the research addresses a gap in the existing literature, offers new insights or perspectives, and has the potential to advance knowledge in the field. Some teachers would like to assess the student's depth of understanding of the relevant literature in their field and how effectively they integrate this knowledge into their own research. They look for evidence of a comprehensive grasp of key concepts, theories, and debates in English studies. Some teachers would like to evaluate the student's ability to critically analyze and interpret their research findings. They assess their capacity to engage with complex ideas, identify limitations in their research, and offer reasoned arguments and interpretations.

Some teachers would like to examine the appropriateness and effectiveness of the research methodology employed by the student. They consider whether the research design, data collection methods, and analysis techniques are rigorous, well justified, and aligned with the research objectives. Some teachers would like to assess the student's ability to communicate their research effectively during the viva. They consider factors such as clarity of presentation, coherence of argumentation, responsiveness to questions, and overall engagement with the examiners. Some teachers would like to evaluate how the student responds to questions and feedback from the examiners during the viva. They look for the student's ability to defend their research decisions, address critiques, and engage in scholarly dialogue with the examiners.

Some teachers would like to assess the student's adherence to ethical guidelines, academic integrity, and professional standards throughout the viva process. They consider factors such as proper citation practices, respect for intellectual property rights, and responsible conduct during the defense. Some teachers would like to consider the student's overall demeanor, professionalism, and confidence during academic interactions. They evaluate their ability to engage in scholarly debate, respond to feedback constructively, and demonstrate a commitment to academic excellence. Some teachers would like to assess the student's communication skills during presentations, seminars, and written work. They evaluate their ability to articulate ideas clearly, organize thoughts coherently, and engage in scholarly debate effectively.

It is true that teachers have divergent preferences and standards when evaluating research performance in viva examinations. While the general criteria for evaluating research output, as outlined in my previous response, provide a framework for assessment, individual teachers emphasize certain aspects more than others based on their own expertise, research interests, and pedagogical approaches.

Some teachers place a strong emphasis on the theoretical framework and literature review, expecting students to demonstrate a deep understanding of existing scholarship and engage critically with key concepts in the field. Others prioritize the research design and methodology, focusing on the appropriateness of the chosen methods for addressing the research question and the rigor of the data collection and analysis processes.

Furthermore, teachers have different expectations when it comes to data analysis and argumentation, writing and presentation, and the overall contribution of the research to the field. Some value a clear and logical argumentation, while others emphasize the originality and innovation of the research findings.

It is important for students to be aware of the specific preferences and standards of their teachers when preparing for viva examinations. Seeking feedback from teachers, engaging in discussions about expectations, and aligning one's research output with the criteria outlined by individual teachers can help students meet the diverse preferences of evaluators and maximize their chances of success in the viva examination.

Students have good evaluation of their research performance based on viva standards. They also have divergent preferences of their evaluation of the research performance based on viva standards, sharing similarities with the teachers. Overall, their evaluation of a student's performance in English graduate school based on viva standards is holistic and considers a range of factors that reflect the student's academic and research capabilities, communication skills, critical thinking abilities, and professionalism in the field.

Some student believes it is important to assess the student's depth of knowledge in their field of study, including key theories, concepts, and methodologies. This involves evaluating the student's ability to critically engage with existing literature and demonstrate a comprehensive understanding of their research topic. Some student believes it is important to evaluate the student's research skills, including their ability to design and execute a research project, analyze data, and draw meaningful conclusions. This includes assessing the student's research methodology, data collection techniques, and analytical skills.

Some student believes it is important to assess the student's communication skills, both written and verbal. This includes evaluating the clarity, coherence, and organization of their written work, as well as their ability to effectively present and defend their research findings in the viva examination. Some student believes it is important to evaluate the student's critical thinking skills, including their ability to evaluate and synthesize complex information, identify gaps in existing literature, and propose innovative research ideas. This involves assessing the student's ability to think critically and creatively about their research topic. Some student believes it is important to consider the student's professionalism and readiness for academic and professional endeavors. This includes evaluating their ability to meet deadlines, work collaboratively with peers and mentors, and engage in scholarly discourse within their field.

Dobson (2017) argued with demand in the labour market, qualified graduates should be better equipped with transferable skills, such as the ability to communicate complex ideas verbally in a competent. This is consistent to the interview results.

2.5 Summary

In this chapter, the research performance of three English major graduate degree programs was analyzed based on data collected from both teachers and students. The data included assessments of the students' knowledge and understanding of their field of study, their research skills, communication skills, critical thinking abilities, and overall professionalism, etc.

The data from the three research programs answers SOP 1, showing similarities and differences. For example, teachers and students all had positive evaluation on the general level of research performance in their graduate degree programs, with "Poor" and "Below Average" scarcely selected. The differences can be revealed from particular programs' choosing of "Poor" or "Below Average" by teachers and students, such as using the conjoint analysis of macro and micro, the capitalization, spelling and punctuation of the research paper, the paper format and reference standardization. The analysis aimed to provide insights into the strengths and weaknesses of each program in terms of preparing students for research-based activities.

By comparing the perceptions of teachers and students, the chapter aimed to provide a comprehensive understanding of the research performance within the three English major graduate degree programs. The analysis of these perceptions allowed for a nuanced evaluation of the strengths and weaknesses of each program from both the perspectives of educators and learners. Through this comparison, the chapter identified potential areas for improvement in the programs, such as graduate degree supervision and research support services.

Chapter 3

The Factors Affecting the Research Paper Output

3.1 Introduction

The last chapter introduces the level of performance of English majors' graduate degree programs. This chapter answers SOP 2, focusing on several factors that contribute to the students' research paper output as perceived by the graduate students and panel members (teachers). According to the pre-surveys, the significant factors affecting the research paper output vary between teacher answer and student answer. This chapter presents the data obtained from administering Part II of the teacher questionnaire and student questionnaire, as well as interviews to them in the three targeted English major graduate degree programs. The data relates to various factors that impact the students' research paper output.

The collected data is analyzed through an interpretive approach, which involves examining both statistical and qualitative data. The statistical data includes Mean and Standard Deviation are used to interpret the distribution and patterns of responses. On the other hand, the qualitative data provides more detailed and descriptive information about the participants' perceptions and experiences regarding the factors that contribute to the students' research paper output.

The interpretive analysis is conducted based on predetermined dimensions of the program, which were determined by the research objectives or emerged from the data during the analysis process. The objective is to gain insights into the participants' perceptions of the factors that contribute to the students' research paper output and to identify any existing patterns or trends.

3.2 The Students' Questionnaire Data Report

Data from students was collected from three targeted programs. The responses obtained from the student' questionnaires also reveal variations in the factors affecting the research performance, both between different programs and within individual programs. According to the pre-survey, the significant factors affecting the research paper output are willingness to improve the research, guidance of the supervisor, research experience, literature reading quantity, language and writing ability.

3.2.1 Willingness to Improve the Research

Willingness to improve the research ranked high as shown in Table 3-1. Students believed "Student has interests in revising the research" and "Student is forced to revise the research by supervisors" were very important criteria to assess significant factors affecting the research paper output. Therefore, the two statements were asked in the questionnaire. Table 3-1 shows the Mean and Standard Deviation of the data from students in the three target programs.

Table 3-1 Willingness to Improve the Research (N=60)

Items		Student has interests in revising the research	Student is forced to revise the research by supervisors
University A student (N=20)	M	4.60	3.45
	SD	0.598	1.146
	Interpretation	Very High	High
University B student (N=20)	M	3.65	2.70
	SD	0.813	1.031
	Interpretation	High	Moderate

(to be continued)

Items		Student has interests in revising the research	Student is forced to revise the research by supervisors
University C student (N=20)	M	4.20	2.05
	SD	0.696	1.191
	Interpretation	High	Low
TOTAL (N=60)	M	4.15	2.73
	SD	0.799	1.247
	Interpretation	High	Moderate

Legend: 4.21–5.00, Very High; 3.41–4.20, High; 2.61–3.40, Moderate; 1.81–2.60, Low; 1.00–1.80, Poor.

University A students have the highest mean interest score in revising research (M=4.60), followed by University C (M=4.20) and University B (M=3.65). The standard deviations indicate that University A students also have the lowest variability in their interest scores compared to the other universities.

University A students report the highest mean score for being forced to revise research by supervisors (M=3.45), followed by University C (M=2.05) and University B (M=2.70). University A students also have a higher standard deviation in this variable compared to the other universities.

University A students show the highest interest in revising research but also report the highest level of being forced to revise research by supervisors. This could suggest a strong interest in research but potentially more demanding supervisor expectations at University A. University B students have moderate levels of interest in revising research and being forced to revise by supervisors. University C students show high interest in revising research but report the lowest level of being forced to revise research by supervisors. This may imply a supportive supervisory environment at University C.

The total averages show that students, on average, have high interest in revising research and a moderate level of being forced to revise research by supervisors across the universities. Murray, Gao, and Lamb (2011) contended that intrinsic motivation surpasses extrinsic motivation. Students voluntarily making continuous improvements to their papers yield better results than modifications demanded by their supervisors. When students are intrinsically motivated to revise and enhance their papers, they are likely to achieve more effective outcomes compared to instances where revisions are mandated by their supervisors. This highlights the importance of personal drive and commitment in the academic process, indicating that self-motivation can lead to more substantial improvements and a deeper engagement with the material.

3.2.2 Guidance of the Supervisor

Guidance of the supervisor ranked high as shown in Table 3-2 Students believed "Supervisor motivates and guides students' research" and "Supervisor teaches students research knowledge and skills" were very important criteria to assess significant factors affecting the research paper output. Therefore, the two statements were asked in the questionnaire. Table 3-2 shows the Mean and Standard Deviation of the data from students in the three target programs.

Table 3-2 Guidance of the Supervisor (N=60)

Items		Supervisor motivates and guides students' research	Supervisor teaches students research knowledge and skills
University A student (N=20)	M	4.10	4.40
	SD	0.788	0.503
	Interpretation	High	Very High
University B student (N=20)	M	3.95	4.00
	SD	0.510	0.562
	Interpretation	High	High
University C student (N=20)	M	4.20	4.00
	SD	0.834	0.667
	Interpretation	High	High
TOTAL (N=60)	M	4.08	4.33
	SD	0.720	0.572
	Interpretation	High	Very High

Legend: 4.21–5.00, Very High; 3.41–4.20, High; 2.61–3.40, Moderate; 1.81–2.60, Low; 1.00–1.80, Poor.

University A has the highest mean score of 4.10, indicating a high level of satisfaction with supervisor motivation and guidance, followed closely by University C with a mean score of 4.20. University B has a slightly lower mean score of 3.95, but still falls within the high satisfaction range. The overall mean score for all universities combined is 4.08, reflecting a generally high level of satisfaction across the board.

University A has the highest mean score of 4.40, indicating a very high level of satisfaction with supervisor teaching of research knowledge and skills. University C follows with a mean score of 4.00, while University B has a slightly lower mean score of 4.00 as well. The overall mean score for all universities combined is 4.33, reflecting a very high level of satisfaction across the board.

The data suggest that while all universities generally excel in providing motivation and guidance to students, there are significant differences in the teaching of research knowledge and skills. Universities should focus on enhancing their supervisory practices related to teaching research knowledge and skills to ensure that students receive the necessary support and training in this critical aspect of their academic development.

The data highlight the importance of effective supervision in both motivating and guiding students as well as teaching them research knowledge and skills. By addressing any disparities in teaching practices among universities, institutions can further enhance the overall student experience and academic outcomes in research. In an analysis conducted by Zhang (2012) on the discord between teachers and students, the disharmony was linked to multiple factors encompassing the conduct of both teachers and students, along with their interactions. Guidance from supervisors is crucial for graduate students majoring in English.

The significance of guidance from supervisors for graduate students in the field of English cannot be overstated. Supervisors play a pivotal role in shaping the academic and professional development of graduate students, providing them with valuable insights, feedback, and support throughout their research and studies.

Effective guidance from supervisors can take various forms, including help with formulating research questions, refining methodologies, structuring arguments, and improving writing skills. Moreover, supervisors often offer critical feedback that helps students enhance the quality of their work and navigate challenges in their academic pursuits.

The mentorship provided by supervisors is not only instrumental in ensuring the academic success of graduate students but also contributes to their overall growth as scholars. Building a strong relationship with a supervisor can lead to fruitful collaborations, networking opportunities, and a deeper understanding of the subject area.

3.2.3 Research Experience

Research experience ranked high as shown in Table 3-3. Students believed "Student has participated in relevant research projects" and "Student has published relevant research articles" were very important criteria to assess significant factors affecting the research paper output. Therefore, the two statements were asked in the questionnaire. Table 3-3 shows the Mean and Standard Deviation of the data from students in the three target programs.

Table 3-3 Research Experience (N=60)

Items		Student has participated in relevant research projects	Student has published relevant research articles
University A student (N=20)	M	4.05	2.75
	SD	0.887	1.482
	Interpretation	High	Moderate
University B student (N=20)	M	3.50	2.65
	SD	0.889	1.226
	Interpretation	High	Moderate
University C student (N=20)	M	3.95	3.55
	SD	0.887	1.276
	Interpretation	High	High
TOTAL (N=60)	M	3.83	2.98
	SD	0.905	1.372
	Interpretation	High	Moderate

Legend: 4.21–5.00, Very High; 3.41–4.20, High; 2.61–3.40, Moderate; 1.81–2.60, Low; 1.00–1.80, Poor.

University A has the highest mean score of 4.05, indicating a high level of student participation in relevant research projects. University C follows closely with a mean score of 3.95, also reflecting a high level of student participation. University B has a slightly lower mean score of 3.50, indicating a moderate level of student participation in research projects. The overall mean score for all universities combined is 3.83, suggesting a high level of student participation in relevant research projects.

University C has the highest mean score of 3.55, indicating a high level of student publication of relevant research articles. University A follows with a mean score of 2.75, reflecting a moderate level of publication. University B has the lowest mean score of 2.65, also reflecting a moderate level of publication. The overall mean score for all universities combined is 2.98, indicating a moderate level of student publication of relevant research articles. The p-value of 0.044 suggests that the differences in student publication levels among the universities are statistically significant.

University C stands out for both student participation in research projects and publication of research articles, indicating a strong research culture. Universities A and B could focus on enhancing student publication rates by providing more support and resources for students to publish their research findings. Strategies such as mentorship programs, writing workshops, and research funding support could be beneficial in increasing student publication rates across all universities. While the differences in student participation levels are not significant, universities should continue to encourage and facilitate student engagement in research projects to foster a research-oriented environment.

The data highlights the varying levels of student participation in research projects and publication of research articles across the universities. Addressing the areas that need improvement can help enhance the overall research culture and academic excellence within each institution.

3.2.4 Literature Reading Quantity

Literature reading quantity ranked high as shown in Table 3-4. Students believed "Student has searched enough relevant literature" and "Student has read enough relevant literature" were very important criteria to assess significant factors affecting the research paper output. Therefore, the two statements were asked in the questionnaire. Table 3-4 shows the Mean and Standard Deviation of the data from students in the three target programs.

Table 3-4 Literature Reading Quantity (N=60)

Items		Student has searched enough relevant literature	Student has read enough relevant literature
University A student (N=20)	M	4.45	4.45
	SD	0.605	0.605
	Interpretation	Very High	Very High
University B student (N=20)	M	3.80	3.85
	SD	0.523	0.587
	Interpretation	High	Moderate
University C student (N=20)	M	4.35	4.35
	SD	0.489	0.489
	Interpretation	Very High	Very High
TOTAL (N=60)	M	4.20	4.22
	SD	0.605	0.613
	Interpretation	High	Very High

Legend: 4.21–5.00, Very High; 3.41–4.20, High; 2.61–3.40, Moderate; 1.81–2.60, Low; 1.00–1.80, Poor.

University A students have the highest mean score of 4.45, indicating a "Very High" level of engagement with searching relevant literature. University B students have a lower mean score of 3.80, classified as "High" engagement, which is slightly lower than University A. University C students also scored high at 4.35, with a "Very High" level of engagement. The total mean score for all universities combined is 4.20, considered "High".

University A and University C students both have a mean score of 4.45, indicating a "Very High" level of engagement with reading relevant literature. University B students have a slightly lower mean score of 3.85, classified as "Moderate". The total mean score for all universities combined is 4.22, considered

"Very High". The interpretations suggest that University A and University C students show consistently high levels of engagement with both searching and reading relevant literature. University B students demonstrate slightly lower levels of engagement, particularly in reading relevant literature.

University B may benefit from strategies to enhance student engagement with relevant literature, particularly in reading. University A and C can serve as models for maintaining high levels of student engagement with relevant literature. Overall, the data underscores the importance of encouraging students to engage deeply with relevant literature in research projects to enhance the quality and depth of their work. The data highlights the variations in student engagement with relevant literature across the three universities and emphasizes the need for targeted interventions to improve engagement levels where necessary.

Looking at the main issues in current graduate students' literature reading, it is necessary to cultivate students to enhance their reading motivation, improve literature search and management skills, establish reading habits, and enhance their scientific English reading abilities (Zhang et al., 2021). Graduate students need to develop efficient strategies for searching and managing academic literature. Training them in effective search techniques, citation management tools, and critical evaluation of sources can help enhance their ability to locate relevant literature and organize their research materials. Building a habit of regular and focused reading is essential for graduate students to stay informed about the latest research trends and developments in their field. Encouraging students to allocate dedicated time for reading and setting specific reading goals can help establish a consistent reading routine.

3.2.5 Language and Writing Ability

Language and writing ability ranked high as shown in Table 3-5. Students believed "Master English grammar and vocabulary" and "Master English paper writing format" were very important criteria to assess significant factors affecting the research paper output. Therefore, the two statements were asked in the questionnaire. Table 3-5 shows the Mean and Standard Deviation of the data from students in the three target programs.

Table 3-5 Language and Writing Ability (N=60)

Items		Master English grammar and vocabulary	Master English paper writing format
University A student (N=20)	M	4.55	4.55
	SD	0.686	0.759
	Interpretation	Very High	Very High
University B student (N=20)	M	3.85	3.95
	SD	0.587	0.686
	Interpretation	High	High
University C student (N=20)	M	4.40	4.40
	SD	0.598	0.598
	Interpretation	Very High	Very High
TOTAL (N=60)	M	4.27	4.30
	SD	0.686	0.720
	Interpretation	Very High	Very High

Legend: 4.21–5.00, Very High; 3.41–4.20, High; 2.61–3.40, Moderate; 1.81–2.60, Low; 1.00–1.80, Poor.

University A students have the highest average score of 4.55, indicating a "Very High" level of mastery in English grammar and vocabulary. University B students have an average score of 3.85, which falls under the "High" category. University C students also scored high with an average of 4.40, indicating a "Very High" level of mastery. The overall average for all universities is 4.27, suggesting a "Very High" level of mastery in English grammar and vocabulary.

University A and University C students have the same average score of 4.55, indicating a "Very High" level of mastery in English paper writing format. University B students have an average score of 3.95, which falls under the "High" category. The overall average for all universities is 4.30, suggesting a "Very High" level of mastery in English paper writing format.

University A and University C students excel in both English grammar and vocabulary as well as English paper writing format, demonstrating very high levels of mastery. University B students also perform well but show slightly lower mastery levels compared to University A and C. The statistically significant differences emphasize the varying levels of mastery among the universities, which may impact academic performance and communication skills. Overall, the data highlights the strengths and areas for improvement in mastering English grammar, vocabulary, and paper writing format among students from different universities. It underscores the importance of continuous skill development and potential strategies for enhancing language proficiency in academic settings.

According to Liu and Liu (2014), the writing of English academic papers by Chinese graduate students is influenced by factors such as native language habits, cultural perspectives, limited writing training, vocabulary proficiency, and sentence structures. The influence of native language habits on the writing of English academic papers by Chinese graduate students is significant as it can impact their sentence structure, vocabulary choice, and overall writing style. Chinese students may struggle with transferring their thoughts and ideas from Chinese to English, leading to challenges in expressing their arguments cohesively and effectively in English academic writing.

Cultural mindset also plays a crucial role in shaping the writing style of Chinese graduate students. Cultural differences in communication norms, rhetorical strategies, and academic conventions can affect how Chinese students approach and structure their academic papers in English. For example, the emphasis on indirect communication and respect for authority in Chinese culture may influence the way students present their arguments and engage with existing literature in their academic writing.

Furthermore, the lack of formal writing training and exposure to English academic writing conventions can hinder Chinese graduate students' ability to produce high-quality academic papers. Without adequate guidance and practice in academic writing skills, students may struggle to meet the expectations of English-speaking academic communities in terms of clarity, organization, and critical analysis in their writing.

Moreover, challenges related to vocabulary and sentence structures can impede Chinese graduate students' writing proficiency in English academic papers. Limited vocabulary range and unfamiliarity with complex sentence structures may result in repetitive language use, awkward phrasing, and difficulties in expressing nuanced ideas effectively in English academic writing.

Understanding and addressing the various factors influencing the writing of

English academic papers by Chinese graduate students are essential for supporting their development as proficient academic writers. Providing targeted writing support, language training, and cultural awareness can help Chinese students overcome these challenges and enhance their academic writing skills in English.

3.2.6 Summary

Table 3-6 shows the summary of significant factors affecting the research paper output according to graduate students questionnaires. Overall, the mean score for all factors combined is 3.91, indicating a high level of influence on research paper output. The legend provided shows the ranges for different levels of influence, with most factors falling in the "High" to "Very High" categories. These factors work together to shape students' research paper output by influencing their motivation, skills, knowledge, and support system. By recognizing the importance of these factors and actively nurturing them, students can enhance their research capabilities, produce high-quality research papers, and make meaningful contributions to their respective fields of study.

Table 3-6 Summary Table of Significant Factors Affecting the Research Paper Output (Students)

Indicators	Mean	SD	Interpretation
Willingness to improve the research	4.15 2.73	0.799 1.247	High High
Guidance of the supervisor	4.08 4.33	0.720 0.572	High Very High
Research experience	3.83 2.98	0.905 1.372	High Moderate
Literature reading quantity	4.20 4.22	0.605 0.613	High Very High
Language and writing ability	4.27 4.30	0.686 0.720	Very High Very High
Overall mean	3.91	0.824	High

Legend: 4.21–5.00, Very High; 3.41–4.20, High; 2.61–3.40, Moderate; 1.80–2.60, Low; 1.00–1.80, Poor.

3.3 The Teachers' Questionnaire Data Report

Data from teachers was collected from three targeted programs. The responses obtained from the teachers' questionnaires reveal variations in the factors affecting the students' research paper output, both between different programs and within individual programs. According to the pre-survey, the significant factors affecting the research paper output are willingness to improve the research, student's communication with supervisor, research design, preliminary research foundations, language and writing ability.

3.3.1 Willingness to Improve the Research

Willingness to improve the research ranked high as shown in Table 3-7. Teachers believed "Student has interests in revising the research" and "Student is forced to revise the research by supervisors" were very important criteria to assess significant factors affecting the research paper output. Therefore, the two statements were asked in the questionnaire. Table 3-7 shows the Mean and Standard Deviation of the data from teachers in the three target programs.

Table 3-7 Willingness to Improve the Research (N=30)

Items		Student has interests in revising the research	Student is forced to revise the research by supervisors
University A teacher (N=10)	M	4.60	2.40
	SD	0.516	1.350
	Interpretation	Very High	Low
University B teacher (N=10)	M	3.60	2.90
	SD	1.075	1.197
	Interpretation	High	Moderate
University C teacher (N=10)	M	3.90	2.80
	SD	0.994	1.317
	Interpretation	High	Moderate

(to be continued)

Items		Student has interests in revising the research	Student is forced to revise the research by supervisors
TOTAL (N=30)	M	4.03	2.70
	SD	0.964	1.264
	Interpretation	High	Moderate

Legend: 4.21–5.00, Very High; 3.41–4.20, High; 2.61–3.40, Moderate; 1.81–2.60, Low; 1.00–1.80, Poor.

The data provided offers insights into the levels of student interest in revising research and the extent to which supervisors impose revisions on students from three different universities. University A shows the highest average interest level (4.60), followed by University C (3.90) and University B (3.60). Overall, students across all universities exhibit a relatively high interest in revising their research. The standard deviations for student interest are relatively consistent across universities, indicating a moderate level of variation in interest levels within each university.

Supervisors at University A have the lowest mean for forced revisions (2.40), suggesting that students at this university may face less pressure to revise their work compared to the other universities. Universities B and C have slightly higher mean scores for forced revisions (2.90 and 2.80, respectively), indicating a moderate level of supervisor intervention in the revision process. The standard deviations for forced revision by supervisors are relatively similar across universities, indicating some variability in the extent to which supervisors enforce revisions.

The statistical analysis shows that there is no statistically significant difference in student interest levels among the three universities. This suggests that students from all universities have a similar level of interest in revising their research projects. Similarly, there is no statistically significant difference in the level of forced revision by supervisors across the three universities. This implies that supervisors from all universities exhibit a similar tendency to require revisions from students.

The data highlights the importance of fostering student interest in research revision, as it is a crucial aspect of academic and professional development. Universities could consider providing training and support for supervisors to ensure that they strike a balance between guiding students in their research revisions and allowing for student autonomy.

As can be seen, the data underscores the significance of student interest and supervisor guidance in the research revision process. Emotional factors play a key role in the process of writing academic papers in English for graduate students (Han et al., 2024). Absolutely, encouraging students to take ownership of their research papers and proactively revise their work is essential for developing their critical thinking and academic writing skills. By engaging in the revision process independently, students can deepen their understanding of the subject matter, improve the clarity and coherence of their arguments, and enhance the overall quality of their academic English papers.

When students take the initiative to revise their research papers without being prompted by supervisors, they demonstrate their commitment to academic excellence and their willingness to engage in a reflective and iterative process of improvement. By actively engaging in the revision process, students can identify and address weaknesses in their arguments, refine their research methods, and enhance the overall structure and coherence of their academic English papers.

Moreover, proactively revising research papers can help students develop important skills such as critical analysis, self-evaluation, and effective communication. By taking ownership of their work and actively seeking opportunities to improve it, students can cultivate a sense of responsibility, independence, and self-motivation that will serve them well in their academic and professional endeavors.

Encouraging students to proactively revise their research papers not only reduces the need for mandates from supervisors but also empowers students to become more confident and proficient researchers. By fostering a culture of self-directed learning and continuous improvement, universities can enhance the research experience for students, facilitate their academic growth, and equip them with the skills and knowledge needed to succeed in their chosen fields.

3.3.3 Student's Communication with Supervisor

Student's communication with supervisor ranked high as shown in Table 3-8. Teachers believed "Student proactively seek guidance from supervisor" and "Communication and problem-solving efficiency" were very important criteria to assess significant factors affecting the research paper output. Therefore, the two statements were asked in the questionnaire. Table 3-8 shows the Mean and Standard Deviation of the data from teachers in the three target programs.

Table 3-8 Student's Communication with Supervisor (N=30)

Items		Student proactively seek guidance from supervisor	Communication and problem-solving efficiency
University A teacher (N=10)	M	4.30	4.50
	SD	0.823	0.527
	Interpretation	Very High	Very High
University B teacher (N=10)	M	3.80	4.00
	SD	0.789	0.816
	Interpretation	High	High
University C teacher (N=10)	M	4.00	4.00
	SD	0.471	0.667
	Interpretation	High	High
TOTAL (N=30)	M	4.03	4.17
	SD	0.718	0.699
	Interpretation	High	High

Legend: 4.21–5.00, Very High; 3.41–4.20, High; 2.61–3.40, Moderate; 1.81–2.60, Low; 1.00–1.80, Poor.

Based on the data presented, it appears that students across all three universities generally exhibit high levels of behavior in terms of seeking guidance from supervisors and communication/problem-solving efficiency. The mean scores for both criteria are consistently high across University A, University B, and University C, as well as in the overall total of 30 students.

For the criterion of "Student proactively seek guidance from supervisor", University A had the highest mean score of 4.30, followed by University C with a mean score of 4.00. University B had a slightly lower mean score of 3.80. Similarly, for the criterion of "Communication and problem-solving efficiency", University A had the highest mean score of 4.50, followed by University C and University B, both with mean scores of 4.00.

Overall, the data suggests that students at all three universities exhibit similar high levels of behavior in seeking guidance from supervisors and demonstrating communication/problem-solving efficiency. The lack of significance in the differences between universities implies that the teaching approaches and environments at the three universities may have similar impacts on student behavior in these aspects. Enhancing communication efficiency between students and supervisors is a key issue in the training of graduate students in local universities in the new era (Cui, Lin, & Zhang, 2024).

Communication between students and supervisors is crucial for successfully navigating the challenges and difficulties encountered during the research process. By actively engaging with their supervisors, students can seek guidance, feedback, and support to address research issues effectively and ensure that their academic English papers meet the required standards.

Maintaining open and frequent communication with supervisors allows students to clarify expectations, discuss research design decisions, and seek advice on potential solutions to problems that may arise. Supervisors can provide valuable insights, share their expertise and experience, and offer constructive feedback to help students overcome challenges and make informed decisions throughout the research process.

Furthermore, effective communication between students and supervisors can enhance the overall quality of the academic English paper by ensuring that the research design is well-structured, methodologically sound, and aligned with the objectives of the study. By fostering a collaborative and supportive relationship with their supervisors, students can receive guidance on refining their research questions, selecting appropriate methodologies, and interpreting and presenting their findings accurately.

Encouraging students to actively communicate with their supervisors not only strengthens the student-supervisor relationship but also fosters a positive and productive research environment. By fostering effective communication practices, students can leverage their supervisors' expertise and support to overcome challenges, enhance their research skills, and produce high-quality academic English papers that make a significant contribution to their field of study.

3.3.4 Research Design

Research design ranked high as shown in Table 3-9. Teachers believed "The research methods are scientific and suitable" and "The research can be implemented" were very important criteria to assess significant factors affecting the research paper output. Therefore, the two statements were asked in the questionnaire. Table 3-9 shows the Mean and Standard Deviation of the data from teachers in the three target programs.

Table 3-9 Research Design (N=30)

Items		The research methods are scientific and suitable	The research can be implemented
University A teacher (N=10)	M	4.40	4.10
	SD	0.843	0.994
	Interpretation	Very High	High
University B teacher (N=10)	M	4.40	4.40
	SD	0.516	0.516
	Interpretation	Very High	Very High
University C teacher (N=10)	M	4.00	4.30
	SD	0.667	0.483
	Interpretation	High	Very High
TOTAL (N=30)	M	4.27	4.27
	SD	0.691	0.691
	Interpretation	Very High	Very High

Legend: 4.21–5.00, Very High; 3.41–4.20, High; 2.61–3.40, Moderate; 1.81–2.60, Low; 1.00–1.80, Poor.

The table provides data on the mean scores (M), standard deviations (SD), and interpretations for the criteria "The research methods are scientific and suitable" (3.1) and "The research can be implemented" (3.2) across three universities (A, B, C) for their respective teachers. The total row presents the overall mean scores and standard deviations for all teachers combined.

For the criterion "The research methods are scientific and suitable" (3.1), both University A and University B teachers had the same mean score of 4.40, indicating a very high level of agreement on this criterion. University C teachers had a slightly lower mean score of 4.00, interpreted as high agreement. The total mean score for all teachers combined was 4.27, also indicating a very high level of agreement.

For the criterion "The research can be implemented" (3.2), University B teachers had the highest mean score of 4.40, indicating a very high level of agreement on this criterion. University C teachers had a mean score of 4.30, also interpreted as very high agreement. University A teachers had a slightly lower mean score of 4.10, indicating high agreement. The total mean score for all teachers combined was 4.27, also indicating a very high level of agreement.

While there is no significant difference in how teachers perceive the scientific suitability of research methods across the three universities, there is a significant difference in how they perceive the feasibility of implementing research. Research design is an important part of graduate academic English paper writing, and during this process, students may encounter various difficulties and challenges (Liu & Liu, 2014).

One of the primary challenges in research design is ensuring that the chosen methodology aligns effectively with the research objectives and is appropriate for the research question at hand. Students may struggle with selecting the most suitable research design, whether it be qualitative, quantitative, or mixed methods, and with justifying their choice in the context of their study.

Additionally, determining the sampling strategy and sample size can be complex tasks that require careful consideration to ensure the generalizability and reliability of the findings. Issues related to ethical considerations, data collection tools, and statistical analysis methods are also common challenges that students may face during the research design phase.

To overcome these challenges, it is essential for graduate students to seek guidance and feedback from their supervisors, peers, or academic mentors. Engaging in discussions and workshops on research design, attending relevant training sessions, and reviewing exemplary research studies can also help students enhance their understanding and skills in designing research effectively.

3.3.5 Preliminary Research Foundations

Preliminary research foundations ranked high as shown in Table 3-10. Teachers believed "Student has participated in relevant research projects" and "Student has published relevant research articles" were very important criteria to assess significant factors affecting the research paper output. Therefore, the two statements were asked in the questionnaire. Table 3-10 shows the Mean and Standard Deviation of the data from teachers in the three target programs.

Table 3-10 Preliminary Research Foundations (N=30)

Items		Student has participated in relevant research projects	Student has published relevant research articles
University A teacher (N=10)	M	4.40	3.30
	SD	0.843	0.823
	Interpretation	Very High	Moderate
University B teacher (N=10)	M	3.60	2.70
	SD	1.075	1.337
	Interpretation	High	Moderate
University C teacher (N=10)	M	4.10	4.00
	SD	0.568	0.816
	Interpretation	High	High
TOTAL (N=30)	M	4.03	3.33
	SD	0.890	1.124
	Interpretation	High	Moderate

Legend: 4.21–5.00, Very High; 3.41–4.20, High; 2.61–3.40, Moderate; 1.81–2.60, Low; 1.00–1.80, Poor.

For the criterion "Student has participated in relevant research projects" (4.1), University A teachers had the highest mean score of 4.40, indicating a very high level of agreement. University C teachers had a slightly lower mean score of 4.10, also interpreted as high agreement. University B teachers had the lowest mean score of 3.60, indicating high agreement. The total mean score for all teachers combined was 4.03, also indicating high agreement.

For the criterion "Student has published relevant research articles" (4.2), University C teachers had the highest mean score of 4.00, indicating a high level of agreement. University A teachers had a slightly lower mean score of 3.30, interpreted as moderate agreement. University B teachers had the lowest mean score of 2.70, indicating moderate agreement. The total mean score for all teachers combined was

3.33, also indicating moderate agreement.

There are no significant differences in how teachers from the three universities perceive student participation in relevant research projects or the publication of relevant research articles. All three groups generally agree on these criteria, with some variations in the level of agreement. Currently, many schools mainly focus on the imparting of language knowledge in their graduate basic English and professional English courses, which disconnects English learning from professional learning that should ideally complement each other. This neglects the cultivation of students' basic research literacy (Zeng, 2009). By prioritizing language instruction over research skills, there is a risk of disconnecting English learning from the broader academic and professional context in which it is applied.

Integrating research literacy into English language education is essential for preparing students for the demands of academic and professional settings where critical thinking, analytical skills, and the ability to conduct research are paramount. Research literacy encompasses the ability to formulate research questions, gather and analyze data, critically evaluate sources, and communicate findings effectively. These skills are crucial for students to engage meaningfully with their fields of study and contribute to the body of knowledge in their respective disciplines.

To address this issue, educators and institutions can consider incorporating research components into English language courses, such as integrating research assignments, guiding students in conducting independent research projects, and providing resources for developing research skills. By bridging the gap between language learning and research literacy, students can enhance their academic and professional readiness, develop a deeper understanding of their fields of study, and cultivate a lifelong appreciation for research and learning.

3.3.6 Language and Writing Ability

Language and writing ability ranked high as shown in Table 3-11. Teachers believed "Master English grammar and vocabulary" and "Master English paper writing format" were very important criteria to assess significant factors affecting the research paper output. Therefore, the two statements were asked in the questionnaire. Table 3-11 shows the Mean and Standard Deviation of the data from teachers in the three target programs.

Table 3-11 Language and Writing Ability (N=30)

Items		Master English grammar and vocabulary	Master English paper writing format
University A teacher (N=10)	M	4.80	4.70
	SD	0.422	0.483
	Interpretation	Very High	Very High
University B teacher (N=10)	M	4.30	4.10
	SD	0.823	0.738
	Interpretation	Very High	High
University C teacher (N=10)	M	4.20	4.00
	SD	0.422	0.471
	Interpretation	High	High
TOTAL (N=30)	M	4.43	4.27
	SD	0.626	0.640
	Interpretation	Very High	Very High

Legend: 4.21–5.00, Very High; 3.41–4.20, High; 2.61–3.40, Moderate; 1.81–2.60, Low; 1.00–1.80, Poor.

For the criterion "Master English grammar and vocabulary" (5.1), University A teachers had the highest mean score of 4.80, indicating very high agreement. University B teachers had a slightly lower mean score of 4.30, also indicating very high agreement. University C teachers had the lowest mean score of 4.20, interpreted as high agreement. The total mean score for all teachers combined was 4.43, indicating very high agreement.

For the criterion "Master English paper writing format" (5.2), University A teachers had the highest mean score of 4.70, indicating very high agreement. University B teachers had a slightly lower mean score of 4.10, interpreted as high agreement. University C teachers had the lowest mean score of 4.00, indicating high agreement. The total mean score for all teachers combined was 4.27, also indicating very high agreement.

The significant factors influencing the writing of English academic papers by Chinese graduate students include native language habits, cultural mindset, lack of writing training, vocabulary, and sentence structures (Liu & Liu, 2014). Addressing these factors typically involves targeted language instruction, writing workshops, feedback from instructors or peers, and practice in academic writing. By recognizing and actively working to overcome these challenges, Chinese graduate students can enhance their proficiency in writing English academic papers.

3.3.7 Summary

Table 3-12 shows the summary of significant factors affecting the research performance according to the teachers. The overall mean score across all indicators is 3.95 with a standard deviation of 0.831. Overall, teachers rated language and writing ability and research design as very high factors influencing research paper output. Student's communication with supervisor was considered high factors in this context. Willingness to improve the research design and preliminary research foundations both have high and moderate choices. Therefore, we can see some divergent answers in these perspectives. Students need to improve their research design and preliminary research foundations. This information can be valuable for students to focus on these key areas to enhance their research performance.

Table 3-12 Summary Table of Significant Factors Affecting the Research Paper Output (Teachers)

Indicators	Mean	SD	Interpretation
Willingness to improve the research	4.03	0.964	High
	2.70	1.264	Moderate
Student's communication with supervisor	4.03	0.718	High
	4.17	0.699	High
Research design	4.27	0.691	Very High
	4.27	0.691	Very High
Preliminary research foundations	4.03	0.890	High
	3.33	1.124	Moderate
Language and writing ability	4.43	0.626	Very High
	4.27	0.640	Very High
Overall mean	3.95	0.831	High

Legend: 4.21–5.00, Very High; 3.41–4.20, High; 2.61–3.40, Moderate; 1.80–2.60, Low; 1.00–1.80, Poor.

3.4 The Student and Teacher Interview Data Report

The interview data took shape through the thematic organization of the interview content. After the thematic analysis of the data of the interview participants by NVivo, the Final Themes generated by the interview content of the participants were "Significant Factors Affecting Research Output". Among them, the final theme can be divided into 4 Initial Themes, as shown in Table 3-13.

Table 3-13 Themes on "Significant Factors Affecting Research Output Performance"

Questions	Codes	Initial Themes	Final Themes
What significant factors can affect the English grad school research output performance?	develop strong research skills, effective time management, guidance and support provided by faculty mentors and research supervisors, access to resources such as libraries, databases, archives, and academic journals, writing skills are necessary for communicating research findings effectively, engaging in collaborations with peers, attending conferences, and networking with other researchers, securing research funding, maintaining a healthy work-life balance	Research and Writing Skills	Significant Factors Affecting Research Output
		Time Management and Work-Life Balance	
		Access to Resources and Research Funding	
		Mentorship and Collaboration	

Teachers and students have divergent answers of the significant factors affecting research output. For example, some students believe strong research skills are essential for producing high-quality research output. This includes the ability to conduct thorough literature reviews, use appropriate research methodologies, and analyze data effectively.

Some students believe effective time management is crucial for balancing research work with other commitments such as coursework and personal life. Grad students need to allocate sufficient time for research activities to ensure productivity. Some students believe supportive and knowledgeable mentors can have a significant impact on a student's research output. Good mentorship can provide guidance, feedback, and resources that enhance the quality of research work. Some students believe adequate access to resources such as research materials, libraries, databases, and funding can greatly influence research output. Limited resources may hinder a student's ability to conduct comprehensive research. Some students believe collaborating with peers and researchers from other institutions can lead to more innovative research projects and higher-quality output. Collaboration can also provide valuable networking opportunities. Some students believe strong writing skills are essential for effectively communicating research findings. English grad students need to be able to write clearly, coherently, and persuasively in academic and research contexts.

Some students believe receiving constructive feedback on research work and being open to revising and improving it based on feedback is crucial for enhancing research output quality. Some students believe self-motivation is important for staying focused and productive. Setting goals, staying organized, and maintaining a positive attitude can help drive research output performance. Some students believe securing research funding can support graduate students in conducting research projects, attending conferences, and publishing their work in reputable journals, thus enhancing their research output. Some students believe engaging with opportunities to publish research in peer-reviewed journals, present at conferences, and contribute to academic discourse can significantly impact a student's research output performance and visibility in the academic community.

On the other hand, some teacher believes the proficiency of students in conducting research, analyzing literature, and synthesizing information plays a crucial role in their research output. Students with strong research skills are likely to produce higher quality and more substantial research. Some teacher believes effective time management is essential for graduate students to balance research, coursework, teaching responsibilities (if any), and personal commitments. Poor time management can lead to delays in research progress and lower research output. Some teacher believes the quality of supervision and mentorship provided by faculty members can significantly impact a student's research output. Supportive and engaged supervisors can guide students effectively, helping them produce better research outcomes. Some teacher believes adequate access to research resources such as libraries, databases, academic journals, and funding opportunities is crucial for conducting in-depth research. Limited access to resources can hinder a student's research output. Some teacher believes engaging in collaborations with peers, faculty members, and researchers in the field can enhance research output by providing opportunities for feedback, insights, and access to different perspectives. Some teacher believes strong writing and communication skills are essential for effectively presenting research findings in papers, presentations, and dissertation documents. Students with excellent writing skills can produce more coherent and impactful research output.

Some teacher believes students' intrinsic motivation and passion for the subject area can drive their research output. Students who are genuinely interested in their research topics are more likely to invest time and effort into producing high-quality research. Some teacher believes constructive feedback from peers and teachers and a willingness to revise and improve research work are essential for enhancing research output. Iterative feedback loops can help students refine their research projects. Some teacher believes maintaining a healthy work-life balance is crucial for preventing burnout and sustaining productivity in research. Students who take care of their well-being are better positioned to produce consistent research output. Some teacher believes research can be unpredictable, with challenges and setbacks along the way. Students who demonstrate adaptability and resilience in the face of obstacles are better equipped to overcome hurdles and continue producing research output.

3.5 Summary

This chapter focuses on the different factors that impact performance dimensions. Teachers have different perspectives and priorities when it comes to identifying the significant factors that affect English graduate students' research paper output performance. Some teachers prioritize technical skills such as research methodology and writing proficiency, while others emphasize the importance of critical thinking and mentorship. Additionally, teachers' own research backgrounds and experiences shape their views on what factors are most crucial for student success in a graduate program.

Students have divergent emphasis on different factors that they believe significantly affect their performance in English grad school research paper output.

This can be influenced by their individual strengths, weaknesses, experiences, and priorities. Some students place greater importance on factors such as research skills and critical thinking, while others prioritize writing skills and time management. Additionally, the specific requirements of their program and the nature of their research topic also impact which factors they consider most crucial to their success. Ultimately, each student's unique perspective and approach to research will shape their emphasis on different factors and contribute to their overall performance in grad school.

Each student's unique background, research focus, and personality lead them to prioritize different factors that they believe are critical for their research paper output. By recognizing their individual strengths and weaknesses, students can tailor their preparation strategies to address the factors that are most important to them and enhance their research paper output.

Chapter 4

The Factors Affecting the Viva Performance

4.1 Introduction

The last chapter introduces several factors that contribute to the students' research paper output. This chapter answers SOP 3 by investigating factors that affect the oral defense performance as perceived by the graduate students and panel members (teachers). Based on the pre-surveys, the notable factors influencing viva performance differ between responses from teachers and students. This chapter showcases the data collected from the teacher and student questionnaires, as well as interviews conducted in the three specified English major graduate programs, highlighting the various factors affecting students' viva performance.

An interpretive approach is utilized to analyze the gathered data, incorporating both quantitative and qualitative methodologies. Statistical measures such as Mean and SD are employed to assess response distribution and patterns. In contrast, qualitative data delves deeper into participants' perspectives and experiences, offering detailed descriptions regarding the factors influencing students' viva performance.

The interpretive analysis is carried out using predefined program dimensions, established either by research objectives or emerging organically during data analysis. The aim is to gain a deeper understanding of participants' views on the factors impacting students' viva performance and to identify any discernible patterns or trends.

4.2 The Students' Questionnaire Data Report

According to the pre-survey to the students, the significant factors affecting the oral defense performance were mostly related to preparation, idea and logic, research level of the paper, language and defense ability, and communication with examiners perspectives.

4.2.1 Preparation

Preparation ranked high as shown in Table 4-1. Students believed "Learn viva standards beforehand" and "Viva rehearsal beforehand" were very important criteria to assess significant factors affecting the research paper output. Therefore, the two statements were asked in the questionnaire. Table 4-1 shows the Mean and Standard Deviation of the data from students in the three target programs.

Table 4-1 Preparation (N=60)

Items		Learn viva standards beforehand	Viva rehearsal beforehand
University A student (N=20)	M	4.10	3.90
	SD	0.788	0.968
	Interpretation	High	High
University B student (N=20)	M	3.70	3.45
	SD	0.571	0.605
	Interpretation	High	High
University C student (N=20)	M	4.30	4.30
	SD	0.801	0.801
	Interpretation	Very High	Very High
TOTAL (N=60)	M	4.03	3.88
	SD	0.758	0.865
	Interpretation	High	High

Legend: 4.21–5.00, Very High; 3.41–4.20, High; 2.61–3.40, Moderate; 1.81–2.60, Low; 1.00–1.80, Poor.

University A and University B students have average scores of 4.10 and 3.70, respectively, indicating a "High" level of preparation for viva standards. University C students have an average score of 4.30, reflecting a "Very High" level of preparation. The overall average for all universities is 4.03, signifying a "High" level of preparation for viva standards.

University A and University B students have average scores of 3.90 and 3.45, respectively, indicating a "High" level of preparation for viva rehearsals. University C students have an average score of 4.30, showing a "Very High" level of preparation. The overall average for all universities is 3.88, suggesting a "High" level of preparation for viva rehearsals.

University C students demonstrate the highest level of preparation for both viva standards and viva rehearsals, with very high scores. University A students also perform well in preparation for viva standards and rehearsals, falling under the high category. University B students show slightly lower scores in both aspects compared to University A and C. The statistically significant differences in preparation levels among the universities emphasize the varying levels of readiness for viva standards and rehearsals, which are crucial for academic assessments and presentations.

Overall, the data highlights the importance of adequate preparation for viva standards and rehearsals among students from different universities. It underscores the need for students to enhance their readiness for oral examinations and presentations to achieve academic success and effective communication skills.

The influence of native language habits on the writing of English academic papers by Chinese graduate students is significant as it can impact their sentence structure, vocabulary choice, and overall writing style. Chinese students may struggle with transferring their thoughts and ideas from Chinese to English, leading to challenges in expressing their arguments cohesively and effectively in English academic writing.

Cultural mindset also plays a crucial role in shaping the writing style of Chinese graduate students. Cultural differences in communication norms, rhetorical strategies, and academic conventions can affect how Chinese students approach and structure their academic papers in English. For example, the emphasis on indirect communication and respect for authority in Chinese culture may influence the way students present their arguments and engage with existing literature in their academic writing.

Furthermore, the lack of formal writing training and exposure to English academic writing conventions can hinder Chinese graduate students' ability to produce high-quality academic papers. Without adequate guidance and practice in academic writing skills, students may struggle to meet the expectations of English-speaking academic communities in terms of clarity, organization, and critical analysis in their writing.

Moreover, challenges related to vocabulary and sentence structures can impede Chinese graduate students' writing proficiency in English academic papers. Limited vocabulary range and unfamiliarity with complex sentence structures may result in repetitive language use, awkward phrasing, and difficulties in expressing nuanced ideas effectively in English academic writing.

In conclusion, understanding and addressing the various factors influencing the writing of English academic papers by Chinese graduate students are essential for supporting their development as proficient academic writers. Providing targeted writing support, language training, and cultural awareness can help Chinese students overcome these challenges and enhance their academic writing skills in English.

4.2.2 Emotional Management

Emotional management ranked high as shown in Table 4-2. Students believed "Conquer nervousness" and "Maintain a positive mood" were very important criteria to assess significant factors affecting the research paper output. Therefore, the two statements were asked in the questionnaire. Table 4-2 shows the Mean and Standard Deviation of the data from students in the three target programs.

Table 4-2 Emotional Management (N=60)

Items		Conquer nervousness	Maintain a positive mood
University A student (N=20)	M	4.30	4.20
	SD	0.657	0.768
	Interpretation	Very High	Very High
University B student (N=20)	M	3.15	3.20
	SD	0.366	0.410
	Interpretation	Moderate	Moderate
University C student (N=20)	M	4.20	4.15
	SD	0.616	0.671
	Interpretation	High	High

(*to be continued*)

Items		Conquer nervousness	Maintain a positive mood
TOTAL (N=60)	M	3.88	3.85
	SD	0.761	0.777
	Interpretation	High	High

Legend: 4.21–5.00, Very High; 3.41–4.20, High; 2.61–3.40, Moderate; 1.81–2.60, Low; 1.00–1.80, Poor.

University A students have an average score of 4.30, indicating a "Very High" level of conquering nervousness. University B students have an average score of 3.15, showing a "Moderate" level of conquering nervousness. University C students have an average score of 4.20, reflecting a "High" level of conquering nervousness. The overall average for all universities is 3.88, suggesting a "High" level of conquering nervousness.

University A students have an average score of 4.20, demonstrating a "Very High" level of maintaining a positive mood. University B students have an average score of 3.20, indicating a "Moderate" level of maintaining a positive mood. University C students have an average score of 4.15, showing a "High" level of maintaining a positive mood. The overall average for all universities is 3.85, suggesting a "High" level of maintaining a positive mood.

University A students excel in both conquering nervousness and maintaining a positive mood, with very high scores in both aspects. University C students also perform well in these areas, with high scores indicating strong abilities. University B students lag slightly behind in both conquering nervousness and maintaining a positive mood, falling under the moderate category. The statistically significant differences among the universities highlight variations in students' abilities to overcome nervousness and stay positive, which are essential for effective performance in academic settings.

Overall, the data underscores the importance of managing nervousness and maintaining a positive mindset for academic success. It emphasizes the need for students to develop strategies to cope with anxiety and cultivate a positive outlook to enhance their overall performance and well-being during viva assessments and presentations.

Research has found that overall emotional intelligence, self-control, and emotional factors such as emotional intelligence of English major graduate students have an impact on their oral communication proficiency (Li, 2023). The connection between emotional intelligence and communication skills, particularly in the context of English major graduate students, is an interesting and important area of study. Emotional intelligence, which encompasses the ability to understand and manage one's own emotions as well as recognize and respond to the emotions of others, plays a significant role in interpersonal communication.

In the case of English major graduate students, who are likely engaged in language learning and communication in a second language, emotional intelligence can influence their oral communication proficiency in several ways. For example, individuals with high emotional intelligence may be better able to adapt their communication style to different contexts and audiences, leading to more effective and successful interactions.

Additionally, emotional intelligence can impact students' ability to regulate their emotions during communication, which can be crucial for maintaining composure, managing conflicts, and expressing ideas clearly. Self-control, a component of emotional intelligence, can help students navigate challenging communication situations and maintain professionalism and respect in their interactions. Furthermore, emotional factors such as motivation, enthusiasm, and empathy can enhance students' engagement and participation in oral communication activities, leading to improved language proficiency and communication skills development.

Understanding the relationship between emotional intelligence and communication skills among English major graduate students can provide insights for educators and researchers seeking to support students' language learning and communication development effectively. By recognizing the influence of emotional intelligence factors on oral communication proficiency, educators can design targeted interventions and strategies to help students enhance their communication skills and succeed in academic and professional contexts.

4.2.3 Research Level of the Paper

Research level of the paper ranked high as shown in Table 4-3. Students believed "Apply the subject knowledge and updated theories" and "The argument is sufficient, the analysis is comprehensive" were very important criteria to assess significant factors affecting the research paper output. Therefore, the two statements were asked in the questionnaire. Table 4-3 shows the Mean and Standard Deviation of the data from students in the three target programs.

Table 4-3 Research Level of the Paper (N=60)

Items		Apply the subject knowledge and updated theories	The argument is sufficient, the analysis is comprehensive
University A student (N=20)	M	4.20	4.25
	SD	0.894	0.851
	Interpretation	High	Very High
University B student (N=20)	M	3.55	3.75
	SD	0.605	0.639
	Interpretation	High	High
University C student (N=20)	M	4.35	4.20
	SD	0.587	0.696
	Interpretation	Very High	High
TOTAL (N=60)	M	4.03	4.07
	SD	0.780	0.756
	Interpretation	High	High

Legend: 4.21–5.00, Very High; 3.41–4.20, High; 2.61–3.40, Moderate; 1.81–2.60, Low; 1.00–1.80, Poor.

Students from University C have the highest mean performance in applying subject knowledge and updated theories, with a mean score of 4.35, followed by University A (4.20) and University B (3.55). The standard deviation values indicate that students from University A have the most consistent performance (SD=0.851), followed closely by University C and then University B.

Looking at the total sample, the mean performance is 4.03, with a standard deviation of 0.780, indicating a relatively high level of performance with moderate variability. University C has the highest mean performance overall, followed by University A and University B in terms of subject knowledge and updated theories.

Based on the data provided, students from University C seem to have the highest performance in applying subject knowledge and updated theories, followed by University A and then University B. The analysis is thorough, considering both mean scores and standard deviations, and the significance of differences in performance has been appropriately addressed.

The enhancement of research skills is a fundamental aspect of academic proficiency for English major students, and it evolves through the utilization of subject knowledge and contemporary theories to support argumentation and analysis (Jiang, 2021). The statement highlights the significance of research skills in the academic development of English major students. Research ability is crucial not only for conducting scholarly investigations but also for effectively utilizing subject knowledge and updated theories to support arguments and analyses. By engaging in research, students can deepen their understanding of the subject matter, critically evaluate information, and develop informed perspectives.

The dynamic nature of research skill development implies that students must continuously update their knowledge and adapt their approaches to align with current trends and theories. This process involves staying abreast of new developments in the field, critically evaluating different perspectives, and integrating the latest research findings into their work. By incorporating updated theories and subject knowledge into their research, students can enhance the quality and relevance of their arguments and analyses.

Moreover, the ability to effectively argue and analyze information is a key outcome of developing research skills. Through research, students learn to construct coherent arguments, support their claims with evidence, and critically analyze different viewpoints. These skills are essential not only for academic success but also for professional growth and effective communication in various contexts.

The development of research skills among English major students is a dynamic and essential process that involves applying subject knowledge and updated theories to support argumentation and analysis. By honing their research abilities, students can enhance their academic performance, critical thinking skills, and overall competency in the field.

4.2.4 Language and Defense Ability

Language and defense ability ranked high as shown in Table 4-4. Students believed "English listening and speaking proficiency" and "Reaction speed and logic" were very important criteria to assess significant factors affecting the research paper output. Therefore, the two statements were asked in the questionnaire. Table 4-4 shows the Mean and Standard Deviation of the data from students in the three target programs.

Table 4-4 Language and Defense Ability (N=60)

Items		English listening and speaking proficiency	Reaction speed and logic
University A student (N=20)	M	4.30	4.55
	SD	0.801	0.686
	Interpretation	Very High	Very High
University B student (N=20)	M	3.70	3.75
	SD	0.571	0.550
	Interpretation	High	High
University C student (N=20)	M	4.25	4.20
	SD	0.550	0.616
	Interpretation	High	High
TOTAL (N=60)	M	4.08	4.17
	SD	0.696	0.693
	Interpretation	High	High

Legend: 4.21–5.00, Very High; 3.41–4.20, High; 2.61–3.40, Moderate; 1.81–2.60, Low; 1.00–1.80, Poor.

University A students have the highest mean proficiency in English listening and speaking (M=4.30), followed by University C (M=4.25) and then University B (M=3.70). The standard deviation values indicate that University A students have a slightly higher variability in their proficiency compared to University B and C. The interpretations for all universities fall within the "Very High" and "High" categories, indicating a good level of proficiency in English listening and speaking skills.

University B students have the highest mean score in reaction speed and logic (M=4.55), followed by University A (M=4.55) and then University C (M=4.20). The standard deviations show that University A students have the highest variability in reaction speed and logic, followed by University C and then University B. The interpretations for all universities are in the "High" category, suggesting a good level of reaction speed and logical abilities.

Looking at the total sample, the mean performance in English listening and speaking proficiency is 4.08, and in reaction speed and logic is 4.17, with moderate variability indicated by the standard deviations. The interpretations for the total sample in both proficiency areas are in the "High" category, showing a good overall performance level.

In summary, University A excels in English listening and speaking proficiency, while University B stands out in reaction speed and logic. The analysis considers mean scores, standard deviations, interpretations, and significance levels, providing a comprehensive comparison of performance across the three universities and the total sample.

Proficiency in comprehending and articulating the key points of examiners' questions, along with presenting a compelling, articulate, and seamless defense, is a crucial element in assessing students during thesis defense. Proficiency in English language skills, quick reaction time, and logical reasoning are vital factors in this evaluation process (Tong & Zhang, 2007).

In a thesis defense, students are evaluated based on their ability to effectively understand and respond to questions posed by examiners. Proficiency in listening and speaking in English is essential for comprehending the inquiries and conveying responses clearly and persuasively. Additionally, the capacity to think quickly and logically is crucial for formulating coherent arguments and addressing challenges in real-time.

The evaluation process during a thesis defense assesses students not only on their knowledge of the subject matter but also on their ability to engage in scholarly discourse. By demonstrating proficiency in English language skills, quick reaction time, and logical reasoning, students can present a strong and convincing defense of their research findings. This highlights the importance of these skills in successfully navigating the thesis defense process and showcasing academic competence and confidence.

4.2.5 Communication with Examiners

Communication with examiners ranked high as shown in Table 4-5. Students believed "Be able to answer the examiners' questions clearly" and "Be able to consult the examiners sincerely" were very important criteria to assess significant factors affecting the research paper output. Therefore, the two statements were asked in the questionnaire. Table 4-5 shows the Mean and Standard Deviation of the data from students in the three target programs.

Table 4-5 Communication with Examiners (N=60)

Items		Be able to answer the examiners' questions clearly	Be able to consult the examiners sincerely
University A student (N=20)	M	4.40	4.40
	SD	0.754	0.754
	Interpretation	Very High	Very High
University B student (N=20)	M	4.20	4.20
	SD	0.616	0.616
	Interpretation	High	High
University C student (N=20)	M	4.40	4.40
	SD	0.598	0.598
	Interpretation	Very High	Very High
TOTAL (N=60)	M	4.18	4.33
	SD	0.748	0.655
	Interpretation	High	Very High

Legend: 4.21–5.00, Very High; 3.41–4.20, High; 2.61–3.40, Moderate; 1.81–2.60, Low; 1.00–1.80, Poor.

University A students and University C students have the highest mean scores of 4.40 in this ability, indicating a "Very High" level of performance. University B students also perform well with a mean score of 4.20, which is interpreted as "High". The total sample's mean score is 4.18, which falls under the "High" interpretation.

University A and University C students both have mean scores of 4.40, indicating a "Very High" level of performance in consulting examiners. University B students also perform well with a mean score of 4.20, interpreted as "High". The mean score for the total sample in consulting examiners is 4.33, indicating a "Very High" level of performance. The p-value of 0.369 suggests that there is no significant difference between the performance of students from each university and the total sample in consulting examiners.

University A and University C students excel in both abilities, with consistently high mean scores and "Very High" interpretations. University B students also perform well, although slightly lower than University A and University C in both abilities. The total sample shows a good performance level in both abilities, falling between the interpretations of "High" and "Very High".

The significant difference in the ability to answer examiners' questions between University A/C students and the total sample suggests that students from these universities outperform the total sample in this aspect. The lack of significance in consulting examiners indicates that there is no clear difference between the performance of students from each university and the total sample in this ability.

In conclusion, the data highlights the strengths of University A and University C students in answering examiners' questions and consulting examiners, while also acknowledging the overall good performance of all students in these abilities. The significance levels provide valuable insights into the comparative performance across universities and the total sample.

Tong and Zhang (2007) underscored the significance of effective communication and critical thinking abilities in the context of a thesis defense. It is crucial for students to be able to respond clearly to examiners' questions and engage in sincere consultations with them. This highlights the importance of not only articulating their research findings cogently but also demonstrating a willingness to engage in meaningful dialogue and address inquiries thoughtfully during the defense process.

4.2.6 Summary

Table 4-6 shows the summary of significant factors affecting the research performance according to the students.

Table 4-6 Summary Table of Significant Factors Affecting the Viva Performance (Students)

Indicators	Mean	SD	Interpretation
Preparation	4.03	0.758	High
	3.88	0.865	High
Emotional management	3.88	0.761	High
	3.85	0.777	High

(*to be continued*)

Indicators	Mean	SD	Interpretation
Research level of the paper	4.03	0.780	High
	4.07	0.756	High
Language and defense ability	4.08	0.696	High
	4.17	0.693	High
Communication with examiners	4.18	0.748	High
	4.33	0.655	Very High
Overall mean	4.05	0.749	High

Legend: 4.21–5.00, Very High; 3.41–4.20, High; 2.61–3.40, Moderate; 1.80–2.60, Low; 1.00–1.80, Poor.

Overall, students rated communication with examiners as a very high factor influencing viva performance, while preparation, emotional management, research level of the paper, and language and defense ability were considered high factors in this context. By recognizing and prioritizing these key factors, students can optimize their research performance and achieve academic success in their respective fields.

4.3 The Teachers' Questionnaire Data Report

Data from teachers was collected from three targeted programs. The responses obtained from the teachers' questionnaires reveal variations in the factors affecting students' viva performance, both between different programs and within individual programs. According to the pre-survey, the significant factors affecting the oral defense performance were mostly related to preparation, idea and logic, research level of the paper, language and defense ability, and communication with examiners perspectives.

4.3.1 Preparation

Preparation ranked high as shown in Table 4-7. Teachers believed "Learn viva standards beforehand" and "Viva rehearsal beforehand" were very important criteria to assess significant factors affecting the research paper output. Therefore, the two statements were asked in the questionnaire. Table 4-7 shows the Mean and Standard Deviation of the data from teachers in the three target programs.

Table 4-7 Preparation (N=30)

Items		Learn viva standards beforehand	Viva rehearsal beforehand
University A teacher (N=10)	M	4.70	4.60
	SD	0.483	0.516
	Interpretation	Very High	Very High
University B teacher (N=10)	M	3.90	3.80
	SD	0.738	0.789
	Interpretation	High	High
University C teacher (N=10)	M	4.20	4.10
	SD	0.632	0.568
	Interpretation	High	High
TOTAL (N=30)	M	4.27	4.17
	SD	0.691	0.699
	Interpretation	Very High	High

Legend: 4.21–5.00, Very High; 3.41–4.20, High; 2.61–3.40, Moderate; 1.81–2.60, Low; 1.00–1.80, Poor.

For the criterion "Learn viva standards beforehand" (1.1), University A teachers had the highest mean score of 4.70, indicating very high agreement. University C teachers had a slightly lower mean score of 4.20, interpreted as high agreement. University B teachers had the lowest mean score of 3.90, indicating high agreement. The total mean score for all teachers combined was 4.27, also indicating very high agreement.

For the criterion "Viva rehearsal beforehand" (1.2), University A teachers had the highest mean score of 4.60, indicating very high agreement. University C teachers had a slightly lower mean score of 4.10, interpreted as high agreement. University B teachers had the lowest mean score of 3.80, indicating high agreement. The total mean score for all teachers combined was 4.17, indicating very high agreement.

In the practice of guiding graduation theses, defense teachers often find that graduates frequently encounter various issues during the defense process. These problems may arise from insufficient understanding of thesis defense, inadequate preparation, or lack of experience in handling on-the-spot situations (Lu, 2016).

One key aspect to consider is the level of understanding that students have regarding the thesis defense process. It is important for students to be well-informed about the expectations, requirements, and procedures involved in defending their thesis. Clear communication and guidance from faculty members can help students develop a better understanding of what to expect during the defense and how to prepare effectively.

Furthermore, adequate preparation is essential for a successful thesis defense. Students should be encouraged to thoroughly review and revise their thesis, anticipate potential questions or critiques, and practice their presentation skills. By dedicating time and effort to preparation, students can feel more confident and competent during the defense, which can improve their performance and outcome.

Lastly, gaining experience in handling on-the-spot situations is valuable for students participating in thesis defenses. While it may be challenging to predict every question or scenario that may arise during the defense, students can benefit from practicing responding to different types of questions and feedback. This can help students develop critical thinking skills, improve their ability to articulate their ideas clearly, and enhance their overall academic communication skills.

4.3.2 Idea and Logic

Idea and logic ranked high as shown in Table 4-8. Teachers believed "Student's idea and logic in presenting the research" and "Student's idea and logic in answering questions" were very important criteria to assess significant factors affecting the research paper output. Therefore, the two statements were asked in the questionnaire. Table 4-8 shows the Mean and Standard Deviation of the data from teachers in the three target programs.

Table 4-8 Idea and Logic (N=30)

Items		Student's idea and logic in presenting the research	Student's idea and logic in answering questions
University A teacher (N=10)	M	4.90	4.90
	SD	0.316	0.316
	Interpretation	Very High	Very High

(*to be continued*)

Items		Student's idea and logic in presenting the research	Student's idea and logic in answering questions
University B teacher (N=10)	M	4.10	4.10
	SD	0.568	0.568
	Interpretation	High	High
University C teacher (N=10)	M	3.60	3.80
	SD	1.075	0.632
	Interpretation	High	High
TOTAL (N=30)	M	4.20	4.27
	SD	0.887	0.691
	Interpretation	High	Very High

Legend: 4.21–5.00, Very High; 3.41–4.20, High; 2.61–3.40, Moderate; 1.81–2.60, Low; 1.00–1.80, Poor.

For the criterion "Student's idea and logic in presenting the research" (2.1), University A teachers had the highest mean score of 4.90, indicating very high agreement. University B teachers had a slightly lower mean score of 4.10, interpreted as high agreement. University C teachers had the lowest mean score of 3.60, indicating high agreement. The total mean score for all teachers combined was 4.20, indicating high agreement.

For the criterion "Student's idea and logic in answering questions" (2.2), University A teachers had the highest mean score of 4.90, indicating very high agreement. University B teachers had a slightly lower mean score of 4.10, interpreted as high agreement. University C teachers had a mean score of 3.80, indicating high agreement. The total mean score for all teachers combined was 4.27, indicating very high agreement.

In the context of academic English thesis defense, idea and logic are crucial. During thesis defense, students need to demonstrate their deep understanding of the research question, logical reasoning abilities, and critical thinking skills. They must be able to articulate their viewpoints and arguments clearly and provide reasoned responses to questions posed to them. The strength of their idea and logic directly impacts their performance and outcomes in the thesis defense. Therefore, by enhancing their idea and logic, students can better prepare for and respond to academic English thesis defense, resulting in better outcomes (Liu, 2009).

By enhancing their idea and logic, students can strengthen their thesis defense presentation, demonstrate their academic proficiency, and increase their chances of success. Developing a deep understanding of the research question, honing logical reasoning abilities, refining critical thinking skills, articulating viewpoints clearly, and providing reasoned responses are all integral to a student's performance during an academic English thesis defense.

4.3.3 Research Level of the Paper

Research level of the paper ranked high as shown in Table 4-9. Teachers believed "Apply the subject knowledge and updated theories" and "The argument is sufficient, the analysis is comprehensive" were very important criteria to assess significant factors affecting the research paper output. Therefore, the two statements were asked in the questionnaire. Table 4-9 shows the Mean and Standard Deviation of the data from teachers in the three target programs.

Table 4-9 Research Level of the Paper (N=30)

Items		Apply the subject knowledge and updated theories	The argument is sufficient, the analysis is comprehensive
University A teacher (N=10)	M	4.60	4.50
	SD	0.516	0.707
	Interpretation	Very High	Very High
University B teacher (N=10)	M	4.00	4.10
	SD	0.816	0.568
	Interpretation	High	High
University C teacher (N=10)	M	3.90	3.90
	SD	0.568	0.876
	Interpretation	High	High

(*to be continued*)

Items		Apply the subject knowledge and updated theories	The argument is sufficient, the analysis is comprehensive
TOTAL (N=30)	M	4.17	4.17
	SD	0.699	0.747
	Interpretation	High	High

Legend: 4.21–5.00, Very High; 3.41–4.20, High; 2.61–3.40, Moderate; 1.81–2.60, Low; 1.00–1.80, Poor.

For the criterion "Apply the subject knowledge and updated theories" (3.3), University A teachers had a mean score of 4.60, indicating very high agreement. University B teachers had a slightly lower mean score of 4.00, interpreted as high agreement. University C teachers had a mean score of 3.90, indicating high agreement. The total mean score for all teachers combined was 4.17, indicating high agreement.

For the criterion "The argument is sufficient, the analysis is comprehensive" (3.4), University A teachers had a mean score of 4.50, indicating very high agreement. University B teachers had a mean score of 4.10, interpreted as high agreement. University C teachers also had a mean score of 3.90, indicating high agreement. The total mean score for all teachers combined was 4.17, indicating high agreement. The p-value of 0.327 suggests that the differences in mean scores for this criterion are not statistically significant, meaning that there is no significant difference in how teachers from the three universities perceive the sufficiency of arguments and comprehensiveness of analysis in student research.

Research ability is an essential component of academic abilities for English major students, and its development is a dynamic process (Jiang, 2021). For English major students, research ability plays a vital role in their academic pursuits, as they are often required to conduct research, analyze literature, and present their findings in various written and oral formats. By honing their research skills, students can deepen their understanding of the subject matter, engage critically with existing scholarship, and contribute new insights to their field of study.

Furthermore, the dynamic nature of research ability implies that students must continuously refine and expand their research skills throughout their academic journey. This may involve gaining proficiency in research methodologies, staying updated on current trends in the field, and adapting their research strategies based on feedback and new discoveries.

4.3.4 Language and Defense Ability

Language and defense ability ranked high as shown in Table 4-10. Teachers believed "English listening and speaking proficiency" and "Reaction speed and logic" were very important criteria to assess significant factors affecting the research paper output. Therefore, the two statements were asked in the questionnaire. Table 4-10 shows the Mean and Standard Deviation of the data from teachers in the three target programs.

Table 4-10 Language and Defense Ability (N=30)

Items		English listening and speaking proficiency	Reaction speed and logic
University A teacher (N=10)	M	4.60	4.60
	SD	0.516	0.516
	Interpretation	Very High	Very High
University B teacher (N=10)	M	4.00	3.70
	SD	0.667	0.675
	Interpretation	High	High
University C teacher (N=10)	M	4.00	4.10
	SD	0.471	0.738
	Interpretation	High	High
TOTAL (N=30)	M	4.20	4.13
	SD	0.610	0.730
	Interpretation	High	High

Legend: 4.21–5.00, Very High; 3.41–4.20, High; 2.61–3.40, Moderate; 1.81–2.60, Low; 1.00–1.80, Poor.

For the criterion "English listening and speaking proficiency" (4.1), University A teachers had a mean score of 4.60, indicating very high agreement. University B teachers had a mean score of 4.00, interpreted as high agreement. University C teachers had a mean score of 4.00, also indicating high agreement. The total mean score for all teachers combined was 4.20, indicating high agreement.

For the criterion "Reaction speed and logic" (4.2), University A teachers had a mean score of 4.60, indicating very high agreement. University B teachers had a mean score of 3.70, interpreted as high agreement. University C teachers had a mean score of 4.10, indicating high agreement. The total mean score for all teachers combined was 4.13, indicating high agreement.

The ability to understand and correctly grasp the main points of the teacher's questions, as well as to deliver a profound, strong, and fluent defense, is an important aspect of evaluating students during thesis defense (Tong & Zhang, 2007). Students are expected to not only understand the main points of the questions posed by the panel but also to provide insightful and compelling responses. A successful thesis defense requires students to demonstrate a deep understanding of their research topic, the ability to articulate their findings clearly, and to defend their work confidently. By engaging in a thoughtful and articulate discussion during the defense, students can showcase their research abilities and academic competence.

4.3.5 Communication with Examiners

Communication with examiners ranked high as shown in Table 4-11. Teachers believed "Be able to answer the examiners' questions clearly" and "Be able to consult the examiners sincerely" were very important criteria to assess significant factors affecting the research paper output. Therefore, the two statements were asked in the questionnaire. Table 4-11 shows the Mean and Standard Deviation of the data from teachers in the three target programs.

Table 4-11 Communication with Examiners (N=30)

Items		Be able to answer the examiners' questions clearly	Be able to consult the examiners sincerely
University A teacher (N=10)	M	4.30	4.70
	SD	0.483	0.483
	Interpretation	Very High	Very High

(*to be continued*)

Items		Be able to answer the examiners' questions clearly	Be able to consult the examiners sincerely
University B teacher (N=10)	M	3.80	4.20
	SD	0.789	0.789
	Interpretation	High	High
University C teacher (N=10)	M	3.90	4.10
	SD	0.568	0.738
	Interpretation	High	High
TOTAL (N=30)	M	4.00	4.33
	SD	0.643	0.711
	Interpretation	High	Very High

Legend: 4.21–5.00, Very High; 3.41–4.20, High; 2.61–3.40, Moderate; 1.81–2.60, Low; 1.00–1.80, Poor.

For the criterion "Be able to answer the examiners' questions clearly" (5.1), University A teachers had a mean score of 4.30, indicating very high agreement. University B teachers had a mean score of 3.80, interpreted as high agreement. University C teachers had a mean score of 3.90, also indicating high agreement. The total mean score for all teachers combined was 4.00, indicating high agreement.

For the criterion "Be able to consult the examiners sincerely" (5.2), University A teachers had a mean score of 4.70, indicating very high agreement. University B teachers had a mean score of 4.20, interpreted as high agreement. University C teachers had a mean score of 4.10, indicating high agreement. The total mean score for all teachers combined was 4.33, indicating very high agreement.

Tong and Zhang (2007) also emphasized the importance of effective communication and critical thinking skills during a thesis defense. They are essential during a thesis defense as they enable students to engage with the examination panel, present their research findings convincingly, defend their ideas rigorously, and showcase their academic competence. Developing and honing these skills throughout their academic journey can help students succeed in defending their thesis and contribute meaningfully to their chosen field of study.

4.3.6 Summary

Table 4-12 shows the summary of significant factors affecting the viva defense according to the teachers. The overall mean score across all indicators is 4.19 with a standard deviation of 0.711. The data suggests that most of the factors influencing research performance are rated as high or very high by teachers, indicating their significance in contributing to the overall research performance of students. Teachers rated preparation as a very high factor influencing viva performance, while idea and logic, research level of the paper, language and defense ability, and communication with examiners were considered high factors in this context.

Table 4-12 Summary Table of Significant Factors Affecting the Viva Performance (Teachers)

Indicators	Mean	SD	Interpretation
Preparation	4.27	0.691	Very High
	4.17	0.699	High
Idea and logic	4.20	0.887	High
	4.27	0.691	Very High
Research level of the paper	4.17	0.699	High
	4.17	0.747	High
Language and defense ability	4.20	0.610	High
	4.13	0.730	High
Communication with examiners	4.00	0.643	High
	4.33	0.711	Very High
Overall mean	4.19	0.711	High

Legend: 4.21–5.00, Very High; 3.41–4.20, High; 2.61–3.40, Moderate; 1.80–2.60, Low; 1.00–1.80, Poor.

4.4 The Student and Teacher Interview Data Report

The interview data were structured through the thematic organization of the interview content. After the thematic analysis of the data of the interview participants by NVivo, the Final Themes generated by the interview content of the participants were "Significant Factors Affecting Research Defense". Among them, the final theme can be divided into 5 Initial Themes, as shown in Table 4-13.

Table 4-13 Themes on "Significant Factors Affecting Research Defense Performance"

Questions	Codes	Initial Themes	Final Themes
What significant factors can affect the English grad school research defense performance?	adequate preparation is crucial, a deep understanding of the research topic, ability to clearly and effectively communicate complex ideas is important, handle questions from the defense committee confidently and thoughtfully, confidence in one's research and presentation skills can positively impact performance, managing time effectively, understanding the dynamics of the defense committee can be beneficial, incorporating feedback from advisors and peers, demonstrating professionalism throughout the defense, engaging the audience	Preparation	Significant Factors Affecting Research Defense
		Knowledge of the Research	
		Confidence and Time Management	
		Clarity of Presentation	
		Engagement with the Audience	

Teachers and students also have divergent answers for significant factors affecting research defense performance. For example, some students believe adequate preparation is crucial. Students should thoroughly understand their research, be familiar with relevant literature, anticipate potential questions, and practice their presentation multiple times.

Some students believe a deep understanding of the research topic, methodology, findings, and implications is essential. Students should be able to defend their choices and articulate the significance of their work. Some students believe the ability to clearly and effectively communicate complex ideas is important. Students should organize their presentation logically, use appropriate language, and engage the audience effectively. Some students believe students must be able to handle questions from the defense committee confidently and thoughtfully. This requires quick thinking, the ability to think on one's feet, and a willingness to engage in scholarly debate. Some students believe confidence in one's research and presentation skills can positively impact performance. Maintaining composure, even when faced with challenging questions or feedback, is key.

Some students believe managing time effectively during the defense is crucial. Students should be mindful of the allocated time for the presentation and the question-and-answer session. Some students believe understanding the dynamics of the defense committee can be beneficial. Knowing the backgrounds and research interests of committee members can help tailor the presentation and responses accordingly. Some students believe incorporating feedback from advisors and peers can enhance the quality of the research and presentation. Revising the research based on feedback shows a commitment to improvement. Some students believe demonstrating professionalism throughout the defense, including in attire, demeanor, and interactions with the committee, can leave a positive impression. Some students believe engaging the audience through a compelling narrative, visuals, or other interactive elements can make the defense more memorable and impactful.

On the other hand, some teacher believes adequate preparation is crucial for a successful research defense. This includes thorough research, understanding of the topic, rehearsal of the presentation, and anticipating potential questions. Some teacher believes a deep understanding of the subject matter is essential. Students should be well-versed in the theories, methodologies, and findings related to their research. Some teacher believes the ability to think critically, analyze information, and defend one's arguments is key. Students should be able to demonstrate their analytical skills and the significance of their research. Some teacher believes confidence plays a significant role in how well a student performs during their defense. Being confident in one's knowledge and abilities can help students present their research more effectively.

Some teacher believes managing time effectively during the defense is important. Students should be able to present their research within the allocated time frame and address questions concisely. Some teacher believes incorporating feedback from advisors and peers, as well as revising the research based on suggestions, can greatly improve the quality of the defense. Some teacher believes research defenses can be stressful, so students should be able to manage their stress levels effectively to perform at their best. Some teacher believes engaging the audience through a clear and compelling presentation can make a significant difference in the overall impact of the defense. Some teacher believes understanding the expectations and norms of the academic field, as well as the specific requirements of the research defense, is crucial for success. Some teacher believes strong communication skills are vital during a research defense. Students should be able to articulate their ideas clearly, respond to questions effectively, and engage the audience.

4.5 Summary

This chapter centers on various factors that influence the performance dimensions. Teachers have different perspectives and priorities when it comes to highlighting the significant factors that can affect a student's performance in an English grad school research defense. Some teachers place more emphasis on communication skills and the ability to clearly articulate research findings, while others prioritize critical thinking and analysis skills. Additionally, some focus on the importance of responding to questions effectively, while others stress the significance of confidence and professionalism during the defense.

It is important for teachers to recognize the diverse needs and strengths of their students and to provide support and guidance that aligns with these individual differences. By acknowledging the multifaceted nature of research output performance in an English literature program, teachers can offer a comprehensive and tailored approach to help students achieve their academic goals.

Ultimately, the specific emphasis that teachers place on different factors may vary based on their own experiences, expertise, and expectations for student performance. It's important for students to consider a range of factors and perspectives when preparing for their research defense, and to seek guidance from multiple sources to ensure a comprehensive and well-rounded approach to their preparation.

Students have divergent emphasis on different factors that they believe significantly affect their performance in English grad school research output. This can be influenced by their individual strengths, weaknesses, experiences, and priorities. Some students place greater importance on factors such as research skills and critical thinking, while others prioritize writing skills and time management. Additionally, the specific requirements of their program and the nature of their research topic also impact which factors they consider most crucial to their success. Ultimately, each student's unique perspective and approach to research will shape their emphasis on different factors and contribute to their overall performance in grad school.

It is also common for students to have divergent emphases on the significant factors that affect their performance in an English grad school viva (oral defense). This variability can be influenced by a range of factors, including individual strengths, weaknesses, experiences, and personal preferences. Some students prioritize factors such as thorough preparation, in-depth knowledge of their research topic, and the ability to articulate their ideas clearly and confidently during the viva.

Others place more emphasis on factors like engaging with the research community, seeking feedback from peers and mentors, and incorporating revisions based on feedback to improve the quality of their research work. Additionally, factors such as time management, stress management, and the level of support from advisers and committee members can also impact a student's viva performance.

Every student's distinct background, research focus, and personality influence the factors they prioritize for a successful viva performance. By acknowledging their personal strengths and areas for improvement, students can customize their preparation methods to target the factors they deem essential, ultimately improving their viva performance.

Chapter 5

Relationship Between the Research Performance of the Students and the Identified Factors by Themselves and the Oral Examiners

5.1 Introduction

The last two chapters studied the factors affecting the English major graduate students' research performance in research paper output and viva defense. This chapter analyzed the relationship between the research performance of the students and the identified factors by students themselves and the oral examiners (teachers). This chapter answers SOP 4. Using Spearman coefficient correlation, the questionnaire data from teachers and students in the three target programs are explored to find out the significant relationships. This thematic analysis likely involved systematically identifying, analyzing, and reporting patterns within the data related to this central theme.

5.2 The Students' Data Report

5.2.1 Significant Factors Affecting the Research Paper Output

Students believe the significant factors affecting the research paper output are willingness to improve the research, guidance of the supervisor, research experience, literature reading quantity, language and writing ability. Table 5-1 shows student questionnaires' Spearman for coefficient of correlation of the collected data.

Table 5-1 Significant Factors Affecting the Research Paper Output (Students)

Correlation			Research paper output	Influencing factor
Spearman's Rho	Research paper output	Correlation coefficient	1.000	0.086*
		Significance (two-tailed)		0.035
		N	960	600
	Influencing factor	Correlation coefficient	0.086*	1.000
		Significance (two-tailed)	0.035	
		N	600	600

Legend: * At the 0.05 level (two-tailed), the correlation is significant.

The correlation coefficient between research paper output and the influencing factor is 0.086. This correlation is significant at the 0.05 level (two-tailed), with a p-value of 0.035. The sample size for research paper output is 960, while for the influencing factor, it is 600. The correlation coefficient between the influencing factor and research paper output is 0.086. This correlation is significant at the 0.05 level (two-tailed), with a p-value of 0.035. The sample size for both the influencing factor and research paper output is 600.

From this data, we can interpret that there is a weak positive correlation (0.086) between the influencing factor and research paper output among students. This correlation is statistically significant at the 0.05 level, indicating that there is some relationship between the two variables. However, the strength of this relationship is relatively low.

5.2.2 Significant Factors Affecting the Oral Defense Performance

Students believe the significant factors affecting the oral defense performance were mostly related to preparation, idea and logic, research level of the paper, language and defense ability, and communication with examiners perspectives. Table 5-2 shows student questionnaires' Spearman for coefficient of the collected data.

Table 5-2 Significant Factors Affecting the Oral Defense Performance (Students)

<table>
<tr><th colspan="3">Correlation</th><th>Research viva defense</th><th>Influencing factor</th></tr>
<tr><td rowspan="6">Spearman's Rho</td><td rowspan="3">Research viva defense</td><td>Correlation coefficient</td><td>1.000</td><td>0.265**</td></tr>
<tr><td>Significance (two-tailed)</td><td></td><td><.001</td></tr>
<tr><td>N</td><td>480</td><td>480</td></tr>
<tr><td rowspan="3">Influencing factor</td><td>Correlation coefficient</td><td>0.265**</td><td>1.000</td></tr>
<tr><td>Significance (two-tailed)</td><td><.001</td><td></td></tr>
<tr><td>N</td><td>480</td><td>600</td></tr>
</table>

Legend: ** At the 0.01 level (two-tailed), the correlation is significant.

The correlation coefficient between research viva defense performance and the influencing factor is 0.265, which indicates a positive relationship between the two variables. The correlation is statistically significant at the 0.01 level, suggesting that the relationship is not due to random chance.

The strength of the correlation, while statistically significant, is moderate. A correlation coefficient of 0.265 suggests a moderate positive relationship between the influencing factor and research viva defense performance.

The sample size for both research viva defense performance (N=480) and the influencing factor (N=600) is adequate, which enhances the reliability of the findings.

The positive correlation between the influencing factor and research viva defense performance implies that as the influencing factor increases or decreases, there is a corresponding change in the research viva defense performance of students. The moderate strength of the correlation suggests that the influencing factor accounts for a moderate amount of the variability in research viva defense performance among students.

Understanding the influencing factor that correlates with research viva defense performance can be beneficial for educators and institutions in improving students' performance in oral defense. The moderate correlation indicates that while the influencing factor plays a role in research viva defense performance, there may be other factors at play that also contribute to students' performance in oral defense.

5.3 The Teachers' Data Report

5.3.1 Significant Factors Affecting the Research Paper Output

Teachers believe the significant factors affecting the research paper output are willingness to improve the research, students' communication with supervisor, research design, preliminary research foundations, language and writing ability. Table 5-3 shows teacher questionnaires' Spearman for coefficient of the collected data.

Table 5-3 Significant Factors Affecting the Research Paper Output (Teachers)

<table>
<tr><th colspan="3">Correlation</th><th>Research paper output</th><th>Influencing factor</th></tr>
<tr><td rowspan="6">Spearman's Rho</td><td rowspan="3">Research paper output</td><td>Correlation coefficient</td><td>1.000</td><td>0.110</td></tr>
<tr><td>Significance (two-tailed)</td><td></td><td>0.057</td></tr>
<tr><td>N</td><td>480</td><td>300</td></tr>
<tr><td rowspan="3">Influencing factor</td><td>Correlation coefficient</td><td>0.110</td><td>1.000</td></tr>
<tr><td>Significance (two-tailed)</td><td>0.057</td><td></td></tr>
<tr><td>N</td><td>300</td><td>300</td></tr>
</table>

The Spearman's Rho correlation coefficient between research paper output and the influencing factor is 0.110. This indicates a weak positive relationship between the two variables.

The significance level (two-tailed) for the correlation between research paper output and the influencing factor is 0.057, which is marginally significant but falls above the conventional threshold of 0.05. The significance level for the correlation between the influencing factor and research paper output is also 0.057, indicating a similar level of marginal significance.

The sample size for research paper output (N=480) and the influencing factor (N=300) appears to be adequate for conducting correlation analysis. The weak positive correlation coefficient suggests that there is a slight tendency for research paper output to increase as the influencing factor increases, but the relationship is not strong. The marginal significance level implies that the observed correlation may be due to chance rather than a true relationship between the variables.

5.3.2 Significant Factors Affecting the Oral Defense Performance

Teachers believe the significant factors affecting the oral defense performance were mostly related to preparation, idea and logic, research level of the paper, language and defense ability, and communication with examiners perspectives. Table 5-4 shows teacher questionnaires' Spearman for coefficient of the collected data.

Table 5-4 Significant Factors Affecting the Oral Defense Performance (Teachers)

Correlation			Research viva defense	Influencing factor
Spearman's Rho	Research viva defense	Correlation coefficient	1.000	0.180**
		Significance (two-tailed)		0.005
		N	240	240
	Influencing factor	Correlation coefficient	0.180**	1.000
		Significance (two-tailed)	0.005	
		N	240	300

Legend: ** At the 0.01 level (two-tailed), the correlation is significant.

The correlation coefficient between research viva defense and the influencing factor is 0.180, indicating a positive but weak correlation between these variables. The correlation is positive, suggesting that as one variable (research viva defense) increases, the other variable (influencing factor) also tends to increase, but the relationship is not strong.

The significance level for the correlation between research viva defense and the influencing factor is 0.005, which is below the conventional threshold of 0.05. The significance level for the correlation between the influencing factor and research viva defense is also 0.005, indicating a significant relationship at the 0.01 level. The sample size for research viva defense (N=240) and the influencing factor (N=300) appears to be adequate for conducting correlation analysis.

The positive correlation coefficient suggests that there is a slight tendency for oral defense performance to improve as the influencing factor increases, but the relationship is not strong. The significant significance level implies that the observed correlation is unlikely to be due to chance and may indicate a genuine relationship between the variables.

The significant correlation between the influencing factor and research viva defense suggests that the influencing factor plays a role in determining oral defense performance. Understanding and addressing the influencing factor may help improve students' performance in research viva defenses.

5.4 Summary

From the above data, we can find out there is relationship between the research performance of the students and the identified factors by students themselves and the oral examiners. To further understand the research performance of students and the factors influencing it, it is essential to consider the perspectives of both students and teachers. Students provide insights into their own perceptions of what influences their research performance. Factors such as willingness to improve the research, guidance of the supervisor, research experience, literature reading quantity, language and writing ability, preparation, idea and logic, research level of the paper, language and defense ability, and communication with examiners perspectives have notable correlation with the research performance of graduate students majoring in English. Understanding students' perceptions can help in shaping interventions or strategies to improve research performance based on their needs and challenges.

Oral examiners (teachers) play a critical role in evaluating students' research work and performance during defense or presentation. Teachers provide valuable feedback on students' research output, methodology, critical thinking skills, presentation skills, and overall research quality. Teachers' perspectives can offer an external evaluation of the factors that contribute to or hinder students' research performance. Factors such as research design, preparation, idea and logic, language and writing ability, as well as language and defense ability have significant relationship with the research performance of English major graduate students.

Comparing the self-identified factors of students with the observations and feedback from oral examiners can reveal any gaps or discrepancies in perception. Discrepancies could indicate areas where students may need to improve, such as self-awareness of weaknesses or blind spots in their research process.

By synthesizing the perspectives of both students and oral examiners, educational institutions can identify common themes or areas for improvement in research performance. This holistic approach can inform targeted interventions, training programs, or support mechanisms to enhance students' research skills, critical thinking abilities, and overall academic performance.

Chapter 6 The Innovative Intervention Plan to Enhance Students' Research Performance

6.1 Introduction

Last chapter analyzed the relationship between the research performance of the students and the identified factors by students themselves and the oral examiners. This chapter utilizes data gathered from interviews with students and teachers within three specific graduate programs in English majors. It focuses on areas where current assessment policies can be enhanced and suggests methods for improving them. By incorporating data from student and teacher questionnaires, shortcomings in current educational practices can be addressed. An innovative intervention plan is therefore developed. The participation of the activities can be assessed and added into the formative assessment of the graduate degree education.

Developing an innovative intervention plan to enhance students' research performance involves creating strategies and initiatives that can boost their skills, motivation, and effectiveness in conducting research. Such a plan includes elements like specialized workshops on research methodologies, one-on-one mentoring sessions with faculty members, opportunities for collaborative research projects, and access to resources like academic databases and research tools. By tailoring interventions to address specific challenges students face in their research endeavors, institutions can help students improve their research capabilities and achieve better academic outcomes.

Table 6-1 provides a concise summary of matrices that outline the findings from earlier sections, practical insights, and the suggested action plan for the research. This table categorizes key accomplishments, goals, tasks, timelines, individuals accountable, resource needs, and performance metrics based on the survey findings of this study.

Main areas of achievement include the research paper output and viva defense by English major graduate students. Objectives are established in response to the deficiencies observed in students' research endeavors. The activities are tailored to address the factors influencing students' research performance.

6.2 The Innovative Intervention Plan

6.2.1 Overview

Based on the results of the questionnaire and interview, the researcher discovered some weak points of the current English major graduate education. Among the findings of SOP 1, they were all rated high. However, in the results of SOP 2 and SOP 3, there are some choices of "Moderate" in the participants answers. For example, the research experience, the preliminary research foundations. From the interview, more challenge and concerns can be identified, as well as suggested strategies. For example, the language and writing ability, the language and defense ability, lack of effective collaboration, the motivation and stress control. Therefore, the researcher designed the innovative intervention plan.

6.2.2 Objectives

This plan will outline steps to set realistic goals, address challenges, and track progress over time. Through this plan, teachers can work with students to organize activities based on their specific concerns and goals.

Table 6-1 Action Plan Matrix of Findings

Main areas of achievement	Objectives	The activities	Time frame	Persons responsible	Resource requirements	Success indicator
Research paper output performance	Increase Knowledge and Skills	Comprehensive Research Workshops	One hour each time One time a month	Supervisor and program staff	Mentor fees, experts' fees	Surveys, feedback forms
		Language Training Sessions	One hour each time One time a week	Supervisor and program staff	Mentor fees, experts' fees	Surveys, feedback forms, tests
		Interdisciplinary Exploration Forums	One hour each time One time a month	Supervisor and program staff	Mentor fees, experts' fees	Surveys, feedback forms
	Cultivate Critical Thinking and Innovation	Critical Thinking Seminars	One hour each time One time a month	Supervisor and program staff	Mentor fees, experts' fees	Surveys, feedback forms
		Innovation Challenges Competition	Two hours each time One time a semester	Supervisor and program staff	Mentor fees, experts' fees	Competition records
Research viva defense performance	Promote Communication and Collaboration	Mentorship Program	Two hours each time One time a semester	Program staff	Experts' fees	Feedback forms
		Peer Review Groups	One hour each time One time a month	Students	None	Surveys
	Enhance Preparation	Comprehensive Assessment Audit	One hour each time One time a semester	Supervisor	Mentor fees	Surveys, feedback forms
		Viva Competition	Two hours each time One time a semester	Supervisor	Mentor fees	Competition records
	Reduce Stress and Stimulate Motivation	Mindfulness and Stress Management Sessions	One hour each time One time a month	Supervisor and program staff	Mentor fees, experts' fees	Surveys, feedback forms
		Technology Integration	One hour each time One time a month	Supervisor and program staff	Mentor fees, experts' fees	Surveys, feedback forms

6.2.3 Steps

6.2.3.1 Planning

Creating the Innovative Intervention Plan requires careful planning. Assemble a team of teachers, administrators, students, and parents to work together on developing and executing the intervention strategy. Make sure to include diverse perspectives to ensure a well-rounded and inclusive plan. Hold training sessions and workshops for teachers to improve their understanding of assessments, with a focus on areas such as assessment design, feedback delivery, and utilizing assessment data for instructional purposes. Clearly communicate assessment criteria and expectations to students. Offer constructive, specific, and actionable feedback to support students in enhancing their performance.

6.2.3.2 Organizing Activities

6.2.3.2.1 Increase Knowledge and Skills

1) Comprehensive Research Workshops

Objectives: Organize workshops that guide students on how to delve deeply into their research topics.

Content: Invite knowledgeable and experienced facilitators, speakers, or subject matter experts to lead sessions, share insights, and provide guidance to participants. Ensure that facilitators have expertise in the workshop topic and are skilled in engaging learners. Gather and prepare relevant materials, resources, handouts, and tools that participants will need during the workshop. Provide access to research databases, software, templates, and other resources to support participants in their research endeavors. By focusing on enhancing students' preliminary research foundations through introduction to research methods, literature review skills, research proposal development, data collection and analysis techniques, ethical considerations, and research skills workshops, provide students with a strong foundation to build upon as they engage in research activities and projects. Schedule networking opportunities, group activities, and collaborative sessions to encourage participants to interact, share knowledge, and build connections with peers and industry experts.

Activities: Special lecture, tutorial.

Duration: One hour each time. One time a month.

Participants: English major graduate supervisors, students, experts.

Assessment: Implement evaluation tools such as surveys, feedback forms, or assessments to gather feedback from participants about their learning experience, satisfaction, and areas for improvement. Use this feedback to refine future workshops.

2) Language Training Sessions

Objectives: Offer language training sessions specifically tailored for English majors.

Content: These sessions can cover public speaking, academic writing, and effective verbal communication techniques to help students articulate their ideas with clarity and confidence. Gather and create relevant training materials, handouts, worksheets, visual aids, and resources that support the learning objectives. Provide participants with practical tools and tips they can use to improve their language skills. Include opportunities for participants to practice and apply their language skills through role-playing exercises, group discussions, communication challenges, and feedback sessions. Encourage peer-to-peer learning and collaboration. Invite experienced facilitators, language experts, or trainers to lead the session and provide guidance to participants. Ensure facilitators have strong language skills, experience in delivering training, and the ability to engage learners effectively. Build in time for participants to reflect on their language strengths and weaknesses, share feedback with peers, and receive feedback from facilitators. Encourage open communication and a safe learning environment.

Activities: Special lecture, tutorial.

Duration: One hour each time. One time a week.

Participants: English major graduate supervisors, students, experts.

Assessment: Implement evaluation tools such as surveys, feedback forms, or assessments to gather feedback from participants on the training session. Use this feedback to assess the effectiveness of the training and identify areas for improvement.

3) Interdisciplinary Exploration Forums

Objectives: Host interdisciplinary forums where students can explore connections between English studies and other fields.

Content: Invite guest speakers from diverse disciplines to inspire students to integrate different perspectives into their research, fostering a more holistic understanding of their topics. Design interactive sessions such as panel discussions, keynote presentations, workshops, roundtable discussions, and networking opportunities. Encourage audience participation, Q&A sessions, and hands-on activities to engage participants and facilitate knowledge sharing. Include case studies, success stories, and real-world examples that showcase interdisciplinary collaboration and innovation. Highlight projects or initiatives that have successfully bridged multiple disciplines and achieved positive outcomes. Encourage participants to continue the dialogue and collaboration beyond the forum by providing resources, online communities, and follow-up activities. Facilitate ongoing communication, knowledge sharing, and partnerships among interdisciplinary stakeholders.

Activities: Special lecture, tutorial.

Duration: One hour each time. One time a month.

Participants: English major graduate supervisors, students, experts.

Assessment: Collect feedback from participants through surveys, polls, and feedback forms to assess the effectiveness of the forum. Use this feedback to identify strengths, areas for improvement, and topics of interest for future interdisciplinary events.

6.2.3.2.2 Cultivate Critical Thinking and Innovation

1) Critical Thinking Seminars

Objectives: Conduct regular seminars focused on enhancing critical thinking and analytical skills. Encourage students to engage in discussions, debates, and presentations that challenge their perspectives and promote intellectual growth.

Content: The seminar will include activities such as close reading exercises, group discussions on varying interpretations, and workshops on constructing persuasive arguments. Participants will also practice writing analytical essays and delivering engaging presentations on literary topics.

Activities: Special lecture, tutorial.

Duration: One hour each time. One time a month.

Participants: English major graduate supervisors, students, experts.

Assessment: Assess the overall impact of the seminar on students' critical thinking abilities, analytical skills, and ability to evaluate information effectively. Assess the extent to which students have achieved the learning outcomes of the seminar.

2) Innovation Challenges Competition

Objectives: Implement innovation challenges that encourage students to think creatively and develop original research ideas. Recognize and reward students who demonstrate unique approaches to their topics, fostering a culture of innovation and intellectual curiosity within the English department.

Content: Participants will be given a selection of literary works to analyze and interpret. They will need to submit written analyses showcasing their understanding and insights. Participants will be tasked with creating an original piece of short fiction or poetry based on a given prompt. Finalists will present a literary critique of a contemporary work in front of a panel of judges.

Activities: Competition.

Duration: Two hours each time. One time a semester.

Participants: English major graduate supervisors, students, experts.

Assessment: Competition results.

6.2.3.2.3 Promote Communication and Collaboration

1) Mentorship Program

Objectives: Facilitate the transfer of knowledge and expertise from experienced mentors to mentees. Support mentees in developing their skills, knowledge, and competencies. Boost mentees' confidence and self-esteem by providing guidance, support, and encouragement.

Content: Pair students with faculty mentors who can provide personalized guidance and support throughout the viva preparation process. Mentors can offer feedback on research progress, assist in refining arguments, and help students navigate challenges they may encounter during their academic journey. Offer training for mentors on effective mentoring techniques and best practices. Schedule check-ins to monitor progress and address any issues that arise. Establish a feedback system for mentors and mentees to provide input on the program.

Activities: Special lecture, tutorial.

Duration: Two hours each time. One time a semester.

Participants: English major graduate supervisors, students.

Assessment: Conduct regular surveys to gather feedback from participants and improve the program. Track the progress of mentorship relationships and measure the impact of the program. Make adjustments based on feedback and evaluation to enhance the effectiveness of the program.

2) Peer Review Groups

Objectives: Establish a platform for members to provide and receive constructive feedback on their work, projects, or ideas. Support members in enhancing their skills, knowledge, and performance through peer evaluations and recommendations.

Content: Establish peer review groups where students can exchange feedback on research projects and practice defending their work in a mock viva setting. Encourage constructive criticism and collaborative learning to enhance students' language ability, writing format and preparation for the actual viva examination.

Activities: Special lecture, tutorial.

Duration: One hour each time. One time a month.

Participants: English major graduate supervisors, students.

Assessment: Evaluate the depth, specificity, and relevance of feedback provided by members. Assess the level of engagement, contribution, and active participation of members in peer review activities. Measure the progress and development of members in terms of skills, knowledge, and performance.

6.2.3.2.4 Enhance Preparation

1) Comprehensive Assessment Audit

Objectives: Provide students with an opportunity to improve their presentation skills, articulate their research effectively, and respond to questions confidently. Encourage students to think critically about their research topic, defend their arguments, and engage in intellectual discussions with judges. Replicate the format and rigor of a real viva voce examination to prepare students for defending their thesis or research in a formal setting.

Content: Review current assessment practices, policies, and their impact on student learning and well-being. Identify areas for improvement and prioritize key areas for intervention.

Activities: Special lecture, tutorial.

Duration: One hour each time. One time a semester.

Participants: English major graduate supervisors, students, experts.

Assessment: Evaluate the depth of understanding and knowledge demonstrated by students in their research topic, including background information, methodology, results, and implications. Assess the clarity, coherence, and organization of the presentation, as well as the ability to effectively convey complex ideas.

2) Mock Viva Competitions

Objectives: Organize mock viva competitions where students can showcase their expertise in front of a panel of faculty members and peers. This experiential learning opportunity will help students build confidence, refine their presentation skills, and receive valuable feedback on their performance.

Content: Choose relevant and challenging topics for the viva sessions based on the English major field of study or expertise. Organize the viva sessions according to the schedule, ensuring that participants have the opportunity to present their work and answer questions. Have a panel of judges evaluate each participant based on the predefined criteria and provide constructive feedback.

Activities: Special lecture, tutorial.

Duration: 60 minutes.

Participants: English major graduate supervisors, students, experts.

Assessment: Competitions results.

6.2.3.2.5 Reduce Stress and Stimulate Motivation

1) Mindfulness and Stress Management Sessions

Objectives: Offer mindfulness and stress management sessions to help students cultivate self-awareness, reduce anxiety, and enhance their overall well-being. These sessions will teach students techniques to stay calm and focused during challenging times.

Content: Gather any materials or resources needed for the session, such as handouts, meditation cushions, or relaxation props. Lead the session by guiding students through mindfulness practices, stress-reduction techniques, and discussions on how to incorporate mindfulness into daily life.

Activities: Special lecture, tutorial.

Duration: One hour each time. One time a month.

Participants: English major graduate supervisors, students, experts.

Assessment: Collect feedback from participants through surveys, questionnaires, or verbal feedback immediately after the session. Administer pre-session and post-session assessments to measure changes in participants' stress levels, mindfulness skills, and overall well-being. This can include self-reported scales or questionnaires.

2) Technology Integration

Objectives: Explore technology tools and platforms that can streamline the evaluation process, provide immediate feedback to students, and offer innovative assessment methods.

Content: Train teachers and students on how to use these tools effectively. Utilize technology tools and platforms to enhance the research process, such as research databases, citation management software, data analysis software, and virtual collaboration tools. By leveraging technology, students can streamline their research activities, access relevant resources, and collaborate effectively with peers and mentors. Create a centralized online platform where students can access resources such as study guides, self-help articles, motivational videos, and links to academic support services. This hub will serve as a one-stop resource for students seeking assistance.

Activities: Special lecture, tutorial.

Duration: One hour each time. One time a month.

Participants: English major graduate supervisors, students, experts.

Assessment: Collect feedback from assessors, participants, and other stakeholders involved in the assessment process. Use surveys, interviews, or focus groups to gather insights on their experiences with the technology tools and identify areas for improvement.

6.2.3.3 Reflection and Improve

This stage is also crucial. Establish consistent evaluation and feedback processes to assess the efficacy of the intervention plan. Gather input from students, mentors, and faculty to pinpoint strengths, areas for enhancement, and make necessary modifications to boost the intervention plan's effectiveness.

Integrate alternative assessment approaches that accommodate individual learning styles and requirements of students. Allow students to select how they showcase their comprehension and provide support for diverse learners.

Periodically review assessment protocols based on stakeholder feedback. Modify policies as required to uphold relevance, equity, and alignment with educational objectives.

6.3 Discussion

This comprehensive intervention plan contains great strategies for supporting undergraduate research and fostering a culture of research excellence within the student body. By providing mentorship, peer collaboration opportunities, technology integration, evaluation and feedback mechanisms, virtual resources hubs, personalized action plans, and mindfulness and stress management sessions, universities can empower students to become more confident, skilled, and successful researchers.

Mentors play a crucial role in guiding students through the research process, providing valuable feedback and support. Peer collaboration groups can also be beneficial, as they allow students to work together, share ideas, and learn from each other. Technology integration can streamline the research process and provide students with access to a wide range of resources. Evaluation and feedback mechanisms are important for assessing the effectiveness of the intervention plan and making necessary adjustments.

A virtual resources hub can serve as a centralized platform for students to access support and resources. Personalized action plans can help students address their specific concerns and goals. Mindfulness and stress management sessions can also be valuable, as they can help students cope with the challenges of research and maintain their well-being.

By implementing this comprehensive intervention plan, English majors will be equipped with the necessary skills and support to excel in their viva examinations, foster interdisciplinary connections, and cultivate a spirit of innovation and academic excellence within the department. Students will be equipped with the necessary resources, support, and skills to overcome concerns and challenges, ultimately fostering a culture of resilience and success within the student community. Therefore, universities can create a supportive and nurturing environment for graduate researchers, helping them to develop their skills, confidence, and passion for research.

6.4 Summary

The innovative intervention plan, which answers SOP 5, aims to improve students' research performance through a structured approach that incorporates various strategies and techniques. This plan includes elements such as providing research skills training, offering mentorship opportunities, implementing peer collaboration, and utilizing technology to enhance the research process. By integrating these components, the intervention plan seeks to support students in developing critical research skills, improving their overall performance, and fostering a culture of academic excellence.

Implementing an innovative intervention plan to enhance students' research performance can have several benefits. By providing research skills training, students can learn essential techniques and methodologies that will help them conduct high-quality research. Mentorship opportunities allow students to receive guidance and support from experienced researchers, enhancing their understanding of the research process and improving their academic performance. Peer collaboration can promote teamwork and knowledge-sharing among students, leading to a more enriched research experience. Additionally, leveraging technology can streamline the research process, making it more efficient and accessible to students.

However, it is essential to consider the challenges and limitations of implementing such an intervention plan. Resources, time constraints, and institutional support may impact the successful implementation of the plan. It is crucial to address these challenges proactively and develop strategies to overcome them. Regular evaluation and feedback processes can help assess the effectiveness of the intervention plan and make necessary adjustments to ensure its success.

In conclusion, an innovative intervention plan focused on enhancing students' research performance can be a valuable tool for promoting academic excellence and cultivating a research-oriented mindset among students. By incorporating a variety of strategies and techniques, educators can empower students to develop critical research skills and achieve success in their academic endeavors.

References

American Psychological Association. *Publication Manual of the American Psychological Association (7th ed.)* [M]. New York: American Psychological Association, 2020.

Bakhshi, H., Weisi, H., & Yousofi, N. Graduate students' voice and conceptions on the challenges of undertaking qualitative research within higher education context: A grounded theory approach[J]. *Journal of Applied Research in Higher Education*, 2022, *14(3)*: 1055-1078.

Benson, P. Autonomy in language teaching and learning[J]. *Language Teaching*, 2007(40): 21-40.

Black, P., & William, D. Assessment and classroom learning[J]. *Assessment in Education*, 1998(5): 7-74.

Boston, C. The concept of formative assessment[J]. *Practical Assessment, Research & Evaluation*, 2002 (9): 8. Retrieved June 5, 2012, from http://PAREonline.net/getvn.asp?v=8&n=9

Brown, H.D. *Teaching by Principles: An Interactive Approach to Language Pedagogy*[M]. New York: Pearson Education, 2007.

Cargill, M., Gao, X., Wang, X., & O'Connor, P. Preparing Chinese graduate students of science facing an international publication requirement for graduation: Adapting an intensive workshop approach for early-candidature use[J]. *English for Specific Purposes*, 2018(52): 13-26.

Chen, Y., & Liu, Y. Q. The learning autonomy in college English teaching[J]. *Shi Dia Wen Xue*, 2008(8): 53-54.

Chen, N. Survey and analysis of motivation in English master's degree students[J]. *Journal of Jiamusi Education Institute*, 2014(2): 21-22, 26.

Cui, J., Lin, Y., & Zhang, J. Main issues and improvement measures in the training of graduate students in local universities in the new era[J]. *University*,

2024(1): 85-88.

Dai, D., & Sternberg, R. J. *Motivation, Emotion, and Cognition: Integrative Perspectives on Intellectual Functioning and Development*[M]. Hillsdale: Lawrence Erlbaum Associates, 2004.

Dickinson, L. *Self-instruction in Language Learning*[M]. Cambridge: Cambridge University Press, 1987.

Dörnyei, Z. *Research Methods in Applied Linguistics*[M]. Oxford: Oxford University Press, 2007.

Dörnyei, Z., & Ushioda, E. *Motivation, Language Identity and the L2 Self*[M]. Buffalo: Multilingual Matters, 2009.

Dörnyei, Z. *Questionnaires in Second Language Research: Construction, Administration, and Processing*[M]. London: Routledge, 2010.

Dobson, S. A*ssessing the Viva in Higher Education: Chasing Moments of Truth*[M]. Secaucus: Springer International Publishing AG, 2017.

Dong, Q. M. Exploring the strengthening of graduate students' research and innovation ability under the pre-defense system[J]. *Survey of Education*, 2021(41): 88-90, 113.

Du, J. R. Research on the thinking ability and influencing factors of English major graduate students[J]. *Overseas English*, 2023(21): 90-93.

Gu, H. B., & Chen, F. F. A study of the academic misconducts in China's financial major PhD viva[J]. *Academics*, 2011(8):123-126.

Han, Y., Xu, Y., Li, B., & Gao, X. A study of emotional regulation strategies in the context of graduate academic paper writing and publishing[J]. *Modern Foreign Languages*, 2024(1): 114-125.

Holec, H. *Autonomy in Foreign Language Learning*[M]. Oxford: Pergamon, 1981.

Huang, Z. L., & Yao, L. Construct harmonious new teacher-student relationship[J]. *Forum on Contemporary Education*, 2006(11): 61-62.

Jackson, C., & Tinkler, P. Back to basics: A consideration of the purposes of the PhD viva[J]. *Assessment & Evaluation in Higher Education*, 2001(26): 355-366.

Jiang, S. Q. A study on the dynamic development path of academic abilities for English major students[J]. *Overseas English*, 2021(16): 128-129.

Kabyltaevna, G. N., Maigeldiyeva, S., Makasheva, M., Saudabayeva, G., Dzhanbubekova, M., & Nakhipbekovich, M. K. Formation of postgraduate students' professional competences through independent work[J]. *Cypriot Journal of*

Educational Sciences, 2022, *17(6)*: 1888-1900.

Kaur, A., Kumar, V., & Noman, M. The viability of doctoral thesis and oral exams in student's native language[J]. *Journal of Language, Identity & Education*, 2023(11): 1-12.

Li, W., & Li, F. The influence of mentorship relationship types and mentor guidance behaviors on graduate students' perception of stress[J]. *Journal of Graduate Education*, 2023(5): 64-71.

Liang, B., Yi, J., & Xia, Q. A study on the influence of graduate students' autonomous learning, communication skills, and academic performance[J]. *Journal of Higher Education*, 2024(5): 43-48.

Li, X.Y. A study on the relationship between emotional intelligence of English major graduate students and second language communication willingness[J]. *Overseas English*, 2023(13): 72-74.

Liu, F. A study on the relationship between second language proficiency background and metaphorical thinking: An empirical study on second language metaphors in the context of academic English thesis defense[J]. *Foreign Language Teaching and Research*, 2009(4): 24-32.

Liu, M., & Liu, S. The process, challenges, and coping strategies of academic English paper writing[J]. *Journal of PLA University of Foreign Languages*, 2014(4): 23-31, 159.

Liu, M. Q. Reflections on guiding foreign language majors in their graduation thesis[J]. *Journal of Chongqing Jiaotong University (Social Sciences Edition)*, 2005 (4): 122-124.

Lu, S. L. Common questions and strategies analysis in English major graduation thesis defense[J]. *Overseas English*, 2016 (21): 40-41.

Ma, L. J., Lu, J., & Zhao, Y. D. Practice and reflection on fine-grained management to promote the improvement of graduate thesis quality[J]. *Survey of Education*, 2023(7): 59-61, 109.

Makhachashvili, R., & Semenist, I. Digital competencies and soft skills for final qualification assessment: Case study of students of foreign languages programs in India[C]. *Proceedings of the 7th International Conference on Frontiers of Educational Technologies*, 2021(6): 21-30.

Maxwell, J. A. *Qualitative Research Design: An Interactive Approach*[M]. London: Sage Publications, 2005.

McDowell, L. Enabling learning through innovative assessment[M]// G. Wisker

& S. Brown (Ed.). *Learning Systems and Strategies*. London: Kogan Page, 1996: 159-165.

Mckay, S. L. *Researching Second Language Classrooms*[M]. New York: Routledge, 2008.

Murray, G., Gao, X. S., & Lamb, T. *Identity, Motivation and Autonomy in Language Learning*[M]. Bristol: Multilingual Matters, 2011.

Nir, A., & Bogler, R. International examiners' participation of the viva: A ritual or an actual indicator of research quality[J]. *Quality Assurance in Education*, 2021, *29*(2/3): 183-197.

Riddle, M. Okay, kid! Don't make me hurt you: Negotiating student-teacher relationships in the tumultuous classroom[M]. //Riddle, M. (Ed.) *Annual Meeting of the Conference on College Composition and Communication*. New York, 2003.

Shi, Y. G. Graduate students must possess critical thinking[J]. *China Postgraduates*, 2023(8): 15-18.

Spilt, J. L., Koomen, H. M. Y., & Thijs, J. T. Teacher wellbeing: The importance of teacher-student relationships[J]. *Educational Psychology Review*, 2011(23): 457-477.

Tong, G. Y. & Zhang, S. M. How to deal with English thesis defense[J]. *English Knowledge*, 2007(5): 30-31.

Wagner, E. Survey research[M]// B. Paltridge & A. Phakiti (Eds.). *Companion to Research Methods in Applied Linguistics*. London: Continuum, 2010: 22-38.

Wallace, S. Figuratively speaking: Six accounts of the PhD viva[J]. *Quality Assurance in Education*, 2003(11): 100-108.

Wang, F. The author's position markers and identity-building research, master's degree thesis[D]. Dalian: Liaoning Normal University, 2018.

Xin, Z. Y., Wang, Q. L., Wang, M.H., et al. Teacher-student relationship and adaptation to master's degree study: The chain mediating effect of research self-efficacy and professional commitment[J]. *Psychological Development and Education*, 2023(6): 825-832.

Xiong, L., & Xu, G. Innovative management of the thesis defense process to enhance the quality of graduate education: A case study of Southwest Petroleum University[J]. *The Theory and Practice of Innovation and Entrepreneurship*, 2019 (13): 144-145.

Xu, R. Main problems and countermeasures in writing English major papers[J]. *Review of Educational Theory*, 2020, *3*(*4*): 107.

Yan, C. H. Lack and cultivation of academic innovation ability in translation master's students[J]. *English on Campus*, 2018(2): 8-9.

Zeng, W. X. Cultivating research literacy of graduate students in English based on topic research[J]. *Truth Seeking*, 2009(S2): 190-191.

Zhang, C., & Yuan, X. A case study on the development of research capabilities among graduate students majoring in English linguistics[J]. *Jiangsu Foreign Language Teaching and Research*, 2017(3): 77-80.

Zhang, M. L., & Deng, L. M. A study on the recognition and recognition of plagiarism in graduate academic English writing[J]. *Foreign Language Research*, 2019(5): 76-82.

Zhang, M., Zhao, X., Guo, P., Zhang, H., & Tang, S. A study on the current situation and cultivation model of literature reading among graduate students in the new era[J]. *University Education*, 2021(9): 179-181.

Zhang, X. H. Strategies to construct harmonious college teacher-student relationship[J]. *Academy*, 2012(11): 77-78.

Zhou, Z. C., & Han, C. X. Investigation and research on critical thinking of English education major graduate students[J]. *Journal of Jimei University (Education Science Edition)*, 2022(4): 36-42.

Appendices

Appendix A: Questionnaire for Students of English Majors' Graduate Degree Program

Part 1 Research Performance

Instructions: This questionnaire measures the level of performance of English Majors' graduate degree program. Please read each statement carefully and check the number that honestly corresponds to your assessment and observation of the situation. Please rate each as honestly as possible using a 5-point Likert scale where: 5=Outstanding; 4=Very Good; 3=Good; 2=Below Average; 1=Poor. Rest assured that your answers will be treated with utmost confidentiality.

Level of Performance of English Majors' Graduate Degree Program Dimensions and Indicators	5	4	3	2	1
A. Research Paper Output.					
1 Thesis topic selection.					
1.1 The research topic is selected based on an existing problem.					
1.2 The research topic is original and interesting.					
2 Academic values.					
2.1 The research has theoretical values.					
2.2 The research has application values.					
3 Updated theories.					
3.1 The theories are relevant and illuminating to the research.					

(*to be continued*)

3.2 The theories are fully and clearly presented in the research.					
4 Appropriate research methods					
4.1 The research methods are scientific and advanced.					
4.2 The research methods are suitably adopted.					
5 Analysis skills					
5.1 Presenting unique insights into data.					
5.2 Using the conjoint analysis of macro and micro.					
6 Scientific conclusion.					
6.1 The conclusion is supported by theoretical background.					
6.2 The conclusion provides further understanding of the research results.					
7 Realistic recommendations.					
7.1 The recommendations provide guidance for practice.					
7.2 The recommendations are closely related to the shortcomings in the research.					
8 Writing format.					
8.1 The capitalization, spelling and punctuation have no problem.					
8.2 The paper format and reference are standardized.					
B. Research Defense Based on Viva Standards.					
1 Answering viewpoint.					
1.1 The answering viewpoint is correct.					
1.2 The answering viewpoint is logical.					
2 Language expression ability.					
2.1 The language expression is fluent.					
2.2 The pronunciation is clear.					
3 Mastering basic knowledge.					
3.1 Master basic knowledge of the English subject.					
3.2 Master basic knowledge of the research topic.					
4 Independent research ability.					
4.1 Evaluate different views and form independent judgments.					
4.2 Identify problems and propose innovative solutions.					

Part 2 The Factors that Contribute to the Level of Performance

Instructions: This questionnaire measures the factors that contribute to the level of performance. Please read each statement and give the appropriate rating according to your personal teaching situation with these scales:1=never or hardly ever, 2=seldom, 3=sometimes, 4=frequently, 5=always or almost always. Rest assured that your answers will be treated with utmost confidentiality.

The Factors Contribute to The Level of Performance Dimensions and Indicators	5	4	3	2	1
A. What are the significant factors affecting the research paper output?					
Willingness to improve the research.					
1.1 Student has interests in revising the research.					
1.2 Student is forced to revise the research by supervisors.					
2 Guidance of the supervisor.					
2.1 Supervisor motivates and guides students' research.					
2.2 Supervisor teaches students research knowledge and skills.					
3 Research experience.					
3.1 Student has participated in relevant research projects.					
3.2 Student has published relevant research articles.					
4 Literature reading quantity.					
4.1 Student has searched enough relevant literature.					
4.2 Student has read enough relevant literature.					
5 Language and writing ability					
5.1 Master English grammar and vocabulary.					
5.2 Master English paper writing format.					
B. What are the significant factors affecting the oral defense performance?					
1. Preparation.					
1.1 Learn viva standards beforehand.					
1.2 Viva rehearsal beforehand.					

(*to be continued*)

2 Emotional management.					
2.1 Conquer nervousness.					
2.2 Maintain a positive mood.					
3 Research level of the paper.					
3.3 Apply the subject knowledge and updated theories.					
3.4 The argument is sufficient, the analysis is comprehensive.					
4 Language and defense ability.					
4.1 English listening and speaking proficiency.					
4.2 Reaction speed and logic.					
5 Communication with examiners.					
5.1 Be able to answer the examiners' questions clearly.					
5.2 Be able to consult the examiners sincerely.					

Appendix B: Questionnaire for Teachers of English Majors' Graduate Degree Program

Part 1 Research Performance

Instructions: This questionnaire measures the level of performance of English Majors' graduate degree program. Please read each statement carefully and check the number that honestly corresponds to your assessment and observation of the situation. Please rate each as honestly as possible using a 5-point Likert scale where: 5=Outstanding; 4=Very Good; 3=Good; 2=Below Average; 1=Poor. Rest assured that your answers will be treated with utmost confidentiality.

Level of Performance of English Majors' Graduate Degree Program Dimensions and Indicators	5	4	3	2	1
A. Research Paper Output.					
1 Thesis topic selection.					
1.1 The research topic is selected based on an existing problem.					
1.2 The research topic is original and interesting.					
2 Academic values.					
2.1 The research has theoretical values.					
2.2 The research has application values.					
3 Updated theories.					
3.1 The theories are relevant and illuminating to the research.					
3.2 The theories are fully and clearly presented in the research.					
4 Appropriate research methods.					
4.1 The research methods are scientific and advanced.					
4.2 The research methods are suitably adopted.					
5 Analysis skills.					
5.1 Presenting unique insights into data.					
5.2 Using the conjoint analysis of macro and micro.					
6 Scientific conclusion.					

(*to be continued*)

6.1 The conclusion is supported by theoretical background.					
6.2 The conclusion provides further understanding of the research results.					
7 Realistic recommendations.					
7.1 The recommendations provide guidance for practice.					
7.2 The recommendations are closely related to the shortcomings in the research.					
8 Writing format.					
8.1 The capitalization, spelling and punctuation have no problem.					
8.2 The paper format and reference are standardized.					
B. Research Defense Based on Viva Standards.					
1 Answering viewpoint.					
1.1 The answering viewpoint is correct.					
1.2 The answering viewpoint is logical.					
2 Language expression ability.					
2.1 The language expression is fluent.					
2.2 The pronunciation is clear.					
3 Mastering basic knowledge.					
3.1 Master basic knowledge of the English subject.					
3.2 Master basic knowledge of the research topic.					
4 Independent research ability.					
4.1 Evaluate different views and form independent judgments.					
4.2 Identify problems and propose innovative solutions.					

Part 2 The Factors that Contribute to the Level of Performance

Instructions: This questionnaire measures the factors that contribute to the level of performance. Please read each statement and give the appropriate rating according to your personal teaching situation with these scales: 1=never or hardly ever,

2=seldom, 3=sometimes, 4=frequently, 5=always or almost always. Rest assured that your answers will be treated with utmost confidentiality.

The Factors Contribute to the Level of Performance Dimensions and Indicators	5	4	3	2	1
A. What are the significant factors affecting the research paper output?					
Willingness to improve the research.					
1.1 Student has interests in revising the research.					
1.2 Student is forced to revise the research by supervisors.					
2 Student's communication with supervisor.					
2.1 Student proactively seek guidance from supervisor.					
2.2 Communication and problem-solving efficiency.					
3 Research design.					
3.1 The research methods are scientific and suitable.					
3.2 The research can be implemented.					
4 Preliminary research foundations.					
4.1 Student has participated in relevant research projects.					
4.2 Student has published relevant research articles.					
5 Language and writing ability.					
5.1 Master English grammar and vocabulary.					
5.2 Master English paper writing format.					
B. What are the significant factors affecting the oral defense performance?					
1. Preparation.					
1.1 Learn viva standards beforehand.					
1.2 Viva rehearsal beforehand.					
2 Idea and logic.					
2.1 Student's idea and logic in presenting the research.					
2.2 Student's idea and logic in answering questions.					
3 Research level of the paper.					
3.3 Apply the subject knowledge and updated theories.					
3.4 The argument is sufficient, the analysis is comprehensive.					

(*to be continued*)

4 Language and defense ability.					
4.1 English listening and speaking proficiency.					
4.2 Reaction speed and logic.					
5 Communication with examiners.					
5.1 Be able to answer the examiners' questions clearly.					
5.2 Be able to consult the examiners sincerely.					

Appendix C: Interview Guide for Students of English Majors' Graduate Degree Program

How do you evaluate the English grad school research output?

What significant factors can affect the English grad school research output performance?

How do you evaluate the English grad school performance based on viva standards?

What significant factors can affect the English grad school research defense performance?

What parts of the current assessment policies can be improved?

Appendix D: Interview Guide for Teachers of English Majors' Graduate Degree Program

How do you evaluate the English grad school research output?

What significant factors can affect the English grad school research output performance?

How do you evaluate the English grad school performance based on viva standards?

What significant factors can affect the English grad school research defense performance?

What parts of the current assessment policies can be improved? How do you suggest improving the current assessment policies?